ABOUT COVER ILLUSTRATION

The cover illustration depicts the Mount Rushmore of Rhode Island's four great sportsmen in our lifetime, Dave Gavitt, Brad Faxon, Billy Andrade and Ben Mondor. The work is by Rhode Island's own nationally syndicated artist/cartoonist Frank Galasso.

The reporter at the foot of the mountain, with notebook in hand ready to work, is Paul Kenyon, the author. Kenyon spent 50 years covering sports in southern New England, the last 37 at the Providence Journal. When he retired in 2014 he had covered more different sports, in more different places, than anyone who has ever worked in Rhode Island.

His book relates memories of some of the games he reported on and the people with whom he worked. It is not as much a sports book as a people book. Kenyon's fascination revolved more around how people act than how they performed in their sport. His anecdotes deal more with human nature than athletic performance.

Kenyon speaks openly about the many reasons he loved his job. One of the more unusual ones is about how his job actually helped save his life in 2000. His assignment was a Patriots-Jets Monday night NFL game. Two of his co-workers, Jim Donaldson and Kevin Mannix, combined with workers at Giants Stadium and, most importantly doctors and nurses at the Hackensack University Medical Center, to save his life. On 9/11/2000 he underwent emergency triple by-pass surgery that saved his life.

In his career, Kenyon was a beat writer for the New England Patriots, the Boston and Pawtucket Red Sox, college basketball, golf and high school sports among many other areas.

It's about the
PEOPLE,
Not Just the Games

50 YEARS COVERING
NEW ENGLAND SPORTS

PAUL KENYON

LifeRich
PUBLISHING

Cover illustration by Frank Galasso

LifeRich Publishing is a registered trademark of
The Reader's Digest Association, Inc.

LifeRich Publishing books may be ordered through booksellers or by contacting:

LifeRich Publishing
1663 Liberty Drive
Bloomington, IN 47403
www.liferichpublishing.com
1 (888) 238-8637

ISBN: 978-1-4897-0809-0 (sc)
ISBN: 978-1-4897-0810-6 (hc)
ISBN: 978-1-4897-0808-3 (e)

Library of Congress Control Number: 2016909611

Print information available on the last page.

LifeRich Publishing rev. date: 06/21/2016

For Pauline Eva, who makes coming home
better than any ball game ever played

CONTENTS

FOREWORD

Billy Andrade and I came of age on the East Bay of Rhode Island long before computers or the internet could give us instant access to all of the statistics available today at a moment's notice.

As young teenagers we were playing a variety of sports, Billy excelled in not only golf, but in baseball and basketball, and he eventually started as a point guard at Providence Country Day, giving up both years and inches to his opponents. He was as good a shooter as he was a putter, if that's even possible. My passions were not only golf, but baseball, hockey and anything with a racquet.

We were a little spoiled back then, our heroes weren't just local sports starts but nationally recognized icons: Bobby Orr, Carl Yastrzemski, John Havlicek and Steve Grogan to name just a few. We worshipped these role models and our most trusted source was our states newspaper, The Providence Journal, or as we like to say in Rhode Island, "the Pro Jo".

As important to us as our local teams and our superstars were the men who wrote about them. Names like Bill Reynolds, Bill Parrillo and Paul Kenyon rolled off our tongues and we both recall getting up early to read the paper before school, OK, maybe I am lying and Billy didn't get up early, but he did like the Evening Journal Bulletin sports section after school!

In August of 1975, I was playing my second time in the Rhode Island State Junior Golf Championship at Pawtucket Country Club. My qualifying score of 73 allowed me to play in the Championship flight where I saw names like Conforti, Vallante, McBride and Marderosian, most of them 2 or 3 years older than me. After a few early wins in my match-play bracket, I was approached by a man with a notepad who introduced himself as Paul Kenyon.

He was soft spoken, polite, inquisitive and asked questions about me. It was my first real interview on the sports scene and I remember it like it was yesterday. He wasn't rushed at all and he looked me in the eye. Paul gripped his pen slightly different than most, and he looked at you while you spoke, writing in some kind of adopted shorthand only decipherable by the writer himself, or perhaps his wife Pauline. Even though he was young, he seemed to know the sport and ask the right kind of questions. There was an immediate and assumed trust in our conversations and to see those conversations get translated into press the next day was a novelty to us. We both cut out the articles and made scrap books that must be hiding in a closet still to this day. There was no question that seeing your name in print aside a picture of oneself was a true motivator that kept us working so that we could see more and more of ourselves in what my father, Brad Faxon, Sr would always say as 'good ink'.

Paul Kenyon was omnipresent. He showed up every week there was a tournament, no matter how big or how small or how far away. He had some innate ability to seemingly ask one or two questions and then right paragraphs or pages on what seemed to be such a simple topic. From day one, Paul would call us from his home phone, which I still have memorized, and ask us not only questions about our own games, but about other competitors we often faced. Those were the glory days where players and scribes had a certain bond and trust on what was on and off the record without having to say it. Paul seemed more interested in our games and rounds than we did ourselves, and he instantly knew how to translate our feelings and emotions into words.

As Paul's career progressed and the newspaper world changed from just print media to all sorts of digital media Paul became more diverse. He was often covering the Patriots, the Red Sox, the Pawsox and almost every high school sport known to man. But selfishly we knew his first love was golf, and when we first turned professional Paul was our favorite guy to speak with because we came of age looking for the Kenyon byline no matter the sport or the time of year. One of Billy's favorite Paul Kenyon stories is from the inaugural CVS/Health Charity Classic back in 1999. Billy had gone to Wake Forest on an Arnold Palmer scholarship, truly the pinnacle of college golf scholarships, and when we began thinking of our first invites to the tournament Arnold was everyone's choice. Paul began writing bio's on all the players (and to this day, it's a favorite among golf aficionados to read his bios) but he really went all out on Arnold, so much so that we thought Paul was in the same foursome as the King himself, and Billy laughs when he hears this and says "no, Paul thought he was Arnold's playing partner!" Paul loved Arnold and like everyone put him on the pedestal that he so richly deserved.

This fantastic community event still is going strong today and without the unfailing dedication that the Providence Journal Sports Department has showed us there is no chance we would have achieved as much in both the national recognition of the states biggest fundraising sporting event or, more importantly, the almost $20 million the event has raised for hundreds of local charities.

Paul Kenyon covered us in the State Juniors, the State Amateur, the New England Amateur, the US Amateur, the US Open, the Masters, the Ryder Cup, the PGA Tour, the Champions Tour, the CVS Health Charity Classic and for 20 years he helped write many pieces covering our Andrade Faxon Charities for Children tournament at Wannamoisett Country Club. We sometime wonder if it weren't for Paul Kenyon would we actually have achieved half of what we actually did? He has been a fixture for us over 41 years and he still has the modesty when he calls to say "Hi, Brad, it's Paul Kenyon." Billy and I feel very blessed and thankful to have come out of this small yet wonderful state, where we were fortunate enough to have matured as not only golfers, but as people. If you ask either one of us who have been some of the most influential people in our fantastic lives, Paul Kenyon's name would be right at the top. It's easy for Rhode Islanders to take for granted Rhode Island Clam Chowder, Del's Lemonade, Narragansett Bay, the PawSox and the beaches of Newport and South County but let's remember how fortunate we are to have had Paul Kenyon at our fingertips for all these years. Thanks Paul for all you have done for us!

Brad Faxon and Billy Andrade

INTRODUCTION

There are special moments in everyone's life that become unforgettable. One that made a huge impact on me came at a most surprising time. I returned home one evening after covering a golf tournament and found Pauline, my wife, reading.

"Anything interesting happen today?" I asked.

"Actually, yes," she responded. "Jayson and I had a very interesting conversation."

Jayson is our younger son. He was a senior in high school at the time and was in the process of deciding where he wanted to go to college. He was wide open, both with where he wanted to go to school and what he wanted to study.

"We were talking, and he told me you were making it hard for him," Pauline said. She said she had the same response I did when she told me. "What are you talking about?" she asked him.

"I can't do what Dad did," he began. "He makes it feel like he never has to work. All he does is go to games. He does what other people do to relax. He likes going to work every day because it is fun for him. That's not the way most people live. I'll never be able to do what he's doing."

Pauline was taken aback. She said she told him he would do just fine with whatever he decided. Later, she thought about what he had said.

"He was right, you know," she told me. "You are pretty lucky."

It stopped me in my tracks. I sat in the den and thought about it. I was proud of my son for being so insightful. And I, too, realized he was absolutely right.

I have been lucky my entire professional career. I had my first story published in the *Pawtuxet Valley Times* when I was a sixteen-year-old sophomore at Bishop Thomas F. Hendricken High School and spent the next fifty years writing for Rhode Island newspapers.

It really was a great way to make a living. It was doubly good for me because another of my fascinations—in addition to sports—is observing and learning from people. For me, the people were as entertaining as the games they played. To this day, my memories, some of which I will relate here, are more about the people than the games.

My career was not by design in many ways. Rather, it was at the direction of my editors that I became the office utility man. I covered Major League Baseball as a full-time beat reporter for two years and as the spare tire to replace a writer with a day off for fifteen more years. That work was split between covering the Major League BoSox and the Triple-A PawSox.

I spent about the same amount of time covering the Patriots and NFL football, again as both the full-time beat man and the day-off replacement. There were occasional trips to the Boston Garden to cover Celtics games and even more rare visits to the same building to report on the Bruins.

The hockey work included working the Stanley Cup finals when they beat Vancouver in 2011, one made memorable for me when I got in trouble for stepping on the spoked-B in the locker room, a definite no-no for superstitious hockey players.

For more than twenty years, the winters revolved primarily around college basketball, which in many ways was even more enjoyable than working with the pros. Rhode Island has a great history with college hoops, and I got to witness it from the press table and the locker room.

I've saved a lot of the game passes, and they line my office wall these days. Super Bowl credentials, World Series badges, the Stanley Cup, the NCAA basketball tournament, the Boston Marathon, a few boxing matches featuring the inimitable Vinny Pazienza, and even the America's Cup sailing races are represented there.

There are passes from the Rainbow Classic in Hawaii, the Golden Harvest Classic in Kansas City, the Cable Car Classic in Santa Clara, the UNO Christmas Tournament in New Orleans, a tournament at Arizona's McKale Center, and one in Kansas City where the University of Rhode Island (URI) played the powerful Kansas Jayhawks.

Most of all, though, there is golf memorabilia. The one constant through it all was golf. Thirteen times to the US Men's Open; the PGA the year Davis Love won under a rainbow at Winged Foot; The Masters twice; the PGA Tour playoffs at the TPC Boston;

many years of PGA Tour events at Pleasant Valley Country Club; a Women's Open at Newport, which turned out to be Annika Sorenstam's final major; and a walking history of the seventeen years CVS has sponsored its Charity Classic at Rhode Island Country Club, hosted by Brad Faxon and Billy Andrade.

I do not think it is unfair to say that I covered more events in more sports in more places than anyone who has ever lived in Rhode Island. I was in the right place at the right time. I was working when the *Providence Journal* began following the state's athletes more than it had ever done before, in part because air travel made it possible, both for the athletes and the reporters.

As Jay said, I really was one lucky guy. What follows are memories of my "working" life.

CHAPTER 1
THE PATRIOTS

For the last several years of my working life, I had a front-row seat to sports history in the making.

As the New England Patriots beat reporter for the *Providence Journal* in Rhode Island, I made the twenty-five-minute trip up Route One four days a week, spent forty-five minutes a day in the team locker room talking to players, and spent another fifteen or twenty minutes listening to the head coach, Bill Belichick, discuss what his team was doing.

Like most reporters, I was too preoccupied with the day-to-day obligations to appreciate the big picture. We spent more time complaining about "The Patriot Way" of doing things, which was to give out information only reluctantly, if at all. Much of the discussion in the media room was built around how our work was more difficult than it needed to be because of the way the team went about its business. As foolish as it sounds now, there were reporters who felt sorry for themselves because they were required to go through this terrible ordeal.

I can laugh about it now. Football writers, under any circumstances, have the most comfortable job in the business. With only one game per week, with clearly defined schedules every other day, and with so many different players and aspects of the game to deal with, working the football beat is as good as it gets.

Covering the Patriots in the twenty-first century has been made even better because of what the team has accomplished. All football fans know about the records the team has compiled under Belichick and quarterback Tom Brady. It is not difficult to make a case that it is the most impressive era by any team in National Football League history and among the most impressive of any sport at any time.

More than the governing body of any other sport, the NFL goes to great lengths to try and establish parity. The Green Bay Packers under Vince Lombardi, the Pittsburgh Steelers under Chuck Noll, and even the San Francisco 49ers under Bill Walsh never had to deal with the league restrictions now in place, from the salary cap to free agency.

The Patriots have established records that might never be equaled. They have been to six Super Bowls and won four. They have been in the AFC championship game nine times. They have had fourteen straight winning seasons, including the only 6-0 regular season in league history. Brady and Belichick have combined to win more games than any coach and quarterback. They have won more playoff games than any coach-quarterback duo in the history of the league.

When a reporter is working every day and concerned with finding something to write about for tomorrow, such accomplishments tend to get lost, which is a shame. Being there every day, though, it was easy to see why the franchise has become so special. I spent at least part of the last twenty years of my career dealing with the Patriots. I was the beat reporter for a total of five years, including 2011–13; in the other seasons, I was the backup for Shalize Manza-Young, Joe McDonald, and Tom E. Curran. All three were outstanding young reporters, as evidenced by the fact that all have gone on to bigger stages.

All of us got to see the team's stadium go from a laughingstock to an ideal twenty-first-century facility, not the most spectacular, to be sure, but more than good enough. It is hard to believe that not long ago, Robert Kraft bought the old stadium for $22 million in bankruptcy court. When he bought the team in 1994, some people criticized him for paying $172 million, the highest price ever paid for a sports franchise at the time in the United States.

By 2016, the team's value was estimated to be $3.2 billion. And that does not include a $375 million shopping and entertainment center built around the $350 million Gillette Stadium. The practice field is adjacent to the south end of the stadium, and an indoor bubble is on the hill next to the practice field. The team has everything it needs at the same site. It is an ideal situation. Put these facilities in the hands of the greatest coach of his generation and the most successful quarterback ever, and everything fell into place to help create football history.

The bad news, of course, is that these achievements came in the midst of controversy, some out of the team's control, but others entirely of its own making.

The Aaron Hernandez situation in 2012 was unbelievable. There is no other word to describe it. The night the Patriots were holding their pre-season dinner with ticket holders, reporters walked over from the press box to the Putnam Clubhouse for a press conference. It turned out the team was announcing the signing of Hernandez, one of its two star tight ends, to a seven-year, $40 million contract extension that included a $12 million signing bonus.

Kraft spoke about how proud he was of Hernandez, who had fallen to the fourth round in the NFL draft because of off-field problems.

"It is one of the most touching moments since I've owned our team. Knowing that this is our charitable gala tonight, Aaron came into my office a little teary-eyed. He presented me with a check to go to the Myra Kraft Giving Back Fund," Kraft said of the charity established in the name of his late wife.

"I said, 'Aaron, you don't have to do this; you've already got your contract.' And he said, 'No, it makes me feel good. I want to do it.'"

The next day in the locker room, I was standing directly in front of Hernandez, my recorder in his face, when he spoke about how he had just had his first child and now had financial security.

"I can't be young and reckless Aaron anymore. I'm going to try to do the right things, be a good father," he said.

Less than a year later, he was charged with murder, eventually convicted, and is now in prison facing more charges. It was a surreal experience, made even harder to believe because at the same time Hernandez was going to jail, Rob Gronkowski, who was taken in the same draft to play the same position, began exploding as one of the biggest stars in the league.

Gronkowski is as advertised, a fun-loving, overgrown kid. He is easy to like. Many people have heard about his outings, but my favorite took place in 2011, before he became really well known. Patriots players are asked to make appearances at charitable events. As part of the team's "Celebrate Volunteerism" program, Gronkowski and his brother, Dan, who was with the Pats as a running back, visited Hope Elementary School in Scituate, Rhode Island.

The brothers presented a ball to Don Campbell, the chief of the Hope Jackson Fire Department, and gave a presentation on fire safety. Gronkowski donned firefighter Kevin Hoskin's full gear and put on a demonstration for the children.

"This is a lot heavier than what we wear on Sunday," Gronkowski told the kids as he struggled to move in the equipment that was a bit too small for him. "I would have a pretty good game if I wore this."

"Rob's a great guy," said Dan Gronkowski, who is four years older than his brother. "He means well with everything he does. He's just always having a good time. Sometimes the media takes it the wrong way. He's a really good guy."

The contrast in the stories of Gronkowski and Hernandez are only part of what seems like a never-ending series of huge events surrounding the Patriots. The questions about whether the Patriots have pushed the limit of the rules, or even broken them, have been another constant surrounding the organization.

The presence of Brady, one of the true superstars in all of sports in the twenty-first century, added to the spotlight on the team, even more so in 2014–15 when Brady, too, was charged with breaking the rules regarding the air pressure in the footballs he used at Gillette Stadium.

It all will go down as one of the wildest sagas in American sports history. And some of us had a front-row seat to all of it. It was a memorable career finale for this reporter.

CHAPTER 2

BILL BELICHICK

If I compiled a list of the most fascinating people I dealt with in athletics, Bill Belichick would be near the top. If I compiled a list of the most frustrating people to work with, Belichick would be near the top of that one, too.

What's more, if I put together a list of the very best coaches I've ever worked with, Belichick would not be near the top. He would *be* at the top, number one, the very best. And I don't think the number-two coach would be anywhere close.

The Patriots coach is one of a kind in so many ways. The team's fans obviously don't worry about the frustrating aspects of his personality. Their only concern is that he has built the Patriots into one of the dominant franchises, not only in the NFL, but in all of sport.

However, those of us who had to meet with him three or four days a week to solicit material for our reports had to deal with his negative aspects. It did not take reporters long to learn what was about to happen when Belichick took over as head coach in 2000.

The team's first preseason contest that year was in the Hall of Fame game held in conjunction with induction ceremonies in Canton, Ohio. The Patriots beat San Francisco in what is, to this day, one of only two games the Patriots have played in July.

The most memorable moments for me came during the pregame meal. About a half dozen New England sportswriters met at one of the large, round tables in the stadium cafeteria. We were having a pleasant time when several of the Cleveland writers came by and joined us.

"Well, do you hate him yet?" one of the Cleveland guys said as he was putting down his tray. He was looking at Nick Cafardo, who at the time was the beat reporter for the *Boston Globe*.

"What are you talking about?" responded Cafardo, who is one of the most even-keeled, level-headed reporters in New England.

"Belichick," the Cleveland writer shot back. "Do you hate him yet? Isn't he the worst?"

Cafardo shrugged uncomfortably and said something about how we were just getting to know him. The Cleveland guy then went into a tirade about how Belichick was so difficult to work with. They told stories about how he was all but run out of Cleveland after five years as head coach in the 1990s, not so much because of a poor record (it was 36–44, with one playoff appearance, which featured a victory over the Patriots), but rather because he had created so many hard feelings not only with the media but with the team's fans, as well. They used words like *surly, prickly,* and *tyrannical* to describe Belichick.

8

As we got to know Belichick, we saw many of the aspects the Cleveland writers told us about. His interview skills—or, perhaps a better way to say it, his willingness to spend fifteen or twenty minutes answering questions—can be awful, as bad as any professional coach in any sport. There are days when you can feel that he wants no part of the process. He wants to get out of there and get back to work.

To his credit, when Belichick took the New England job, he knew that he was not good dealing with the public aspects of the job. He took an unusual step to try and improve in that area. He became one of the first NFL coaches ever to hire a personal public relations person, someone who would work directly for him, not the team.

Berj Najarian, a Boston University graduate, had gotten to know Belichick as a member of the Jets' PR department when Belichick was an assistant there before taking the Patriots job. Najarian was given the title of executive administrator to the head coach. His duties included arranging the coach's public speaking schedule, handling personal requests made to Belichick, and helping with various football and stadium operations.

Another aspect of his work was to prepare the coach for what questions might be asked at his press conference. Najarian would monitor stories in newspapers, radio, and television (there was no Internet then) and do what he could to prep the coach, much as is done for politicians.

Still another aspect was mentoring the players on what to say when they were interviewed. Several times, players left booklets in their lockers that dealt with the Patriots way of doing things. Not only does Belichick only reluctantly give out any information about his team; he demands that his players do the same.

Many Patriot fans might never have heard about Najarian, but he probably has spent more time with Belichick since coming along with him to New England than anyone, including Tom Brady. Najarian often seems like Belichick's shadow. He attends all the press conferences, although he does it very much in the background. He sometimes is in the locker room observing what is happening and how players deal with interviews.

Players must do as they are told or they get in trouble. The style is to never say anything bad about an opponent, never provide any bulletin material, and never divulge any details of the game plan for that week. The preferred response is to simply say, "I'm just trying to get better every day."

At times, it almost gets comical, because the same answer is given to so many different questions. Some players handle it better than others. Ras-I Dowling, a cornerback who was a second-round draft failure, was a classic case of someone who struggled.

He came to Foxboro for the first time immediately after the draft, as all draft picks do. The University of Virginia product made a favorable impression. He was dressed in suit and tie. He was articulate and pleasant to speak with.

Fast forward three months to the start of training camp. The first time Dowling was asked to speak with reporters, he was visibly nervous, clearly uncomfortable. Someone asked how he was feeling as he recovered from injuries that had sidelined him at UVA.

"I'm just trying to get better every day," he said.

There was another question, then a third. The answers were exactly the same. No matter what he was asked, he spit back,

"I'm just trying to get better every day." Obviously, he wanted no part of this. He was worried about getting in trouble. So, after the third question, one of the reporters said, "That's all right Ras-I. We won't bother you." That was the end of the interview, and no one was happier than Dowling.

What Belichick does is identify players who can walk the fine line of answering questions without saying anything of real value and let them serve as spokesmen. Vince Wilfork was one of the main men for many years. Tedy Bruschi was, too, along with Rodney Harrison. More recently, guys like Devon McCourty, Rob Ninkovich, and Jerod Mayo have carried the interview ball.

Najarian obviously has done his job well. In 2005, he was given the title of Patriots executive administrator to the head coach.

Najarian is part of a staff Belichick hand-picks to make sure there is only one real voice in Patriot Nation. It is typical in the NFL for former players to take jobs as assistant coaches. It simply makes sense. They have played the game. They have seen how work is carried out. Most coaches want former players on their staff.

Under Belichick, the Patriots have been different. Pepper Johnson, the former Giant, was a key aide, but he was the exception. Belichick obviously prefers to train his assistants to do things his way and not worry about how others might do it. He not only has precious few former players; his staff is dominated by guys who went to small schools who were not exposed to big-time football, even in college.

Josh McDaniels, the offensive coordinator, went to John Carroll University. Matt Patricia, the defensive coordinator, has an aeronautical engineering degree from RPI. Brian Daboll attended the University of Rochester. Line coach Dave DeGuglielmo is a

Boston University grad. Cornerback coach Josh Boyer went to Muskingum.

Belichick doesn't require a background as a player, but rather a willingness to work long hours and follow The Patriot Way. The coaches are not unlike the players. In the rare times when they are interviewed, they tend to be bland and tight with information, just as the players are required to be. Najarian often is there to monitor their words, as well, although in this day and age, recordings are so commonplace that there is no need to be there in person. They can simply watch the video or replay the tape.

The frustrating part for reporters is that when he is in the mood—which most often means when the conversation does not directly involve his team or its opponent that week—Belichick can be terrific. He is a walking history book on the NFL throughout the last forty years. He knows just about everyone and seems to remember just about everything.

He can be professorial and even spellbinding when he wants to be. Those days often happened on a Friday. By then, the game plan is put in place. The hard work is over, and the last forty-eight hours before a game are more focused on finishing touches than on making major changes. By then, most media members have gathered the information they need, so everything is more relaxed.

On a typical Wednesday, there would be as many as one hundred reporters at the press conferences and twenty cameras or more. Thursday, those numbers typically get cut in half. On Friday, they might be cut in half again. So the Friday sessions tended to be more relaxed.

Several years into his term as coach, the guys who worked for Patriots Football Weekly took over the Friday sessions. First, Bryan Morry and Paul Perillo, and in later years, Perillo, Andy Hart, and Eric Scalavino, would treat Belichick more like a teacher than a coach. Rather than the upcoming opponents, or questions about Patriots injuries (which he never answered on any day), they would ask about trends in the game.

One day, it might have been about the evolution of the tight-end position—the Patriots had Rob Gronkowski and Aaron Hernandez and used them unlike any pair of tight ends in NFL history. Another day, it might be about the strengths and weaknesses of a 4–3 defensive, rather than a 3–4.

One of the days I most enjoyed was when the issue of the alignment of the punt team was brought up. Belichick, of course, worked as a special teams coach early in his career. The subject brought out the best in him. He went into a five-minute dissertation revolving around Steve DeOssie, the former Patriot and Giant who now does media work in Boston, and his son, Zak, a Brown grad who was with the Giants as a Pro Bowl long snapper.

Belichick sounded as if he was delivering a lecture as he spoke off the top of his head.

"In a lot of respects, Steve really changed … in my opinion, he changed the punting game in the National Football League and ultimately in college as well," Belichick said.

Until the 1990s, the player who snapped the ball for a punt or field goal was someone who played another position, often a center, but not necessarily. Steve DeOssie, a Boston College grad who was a linebacker by trade, was an example.

"I'd say up until that point, it was usually nine against ten," Belichick pointed out. "You only had nine blockers—the center wasn't responsible for a man—so you had nine blockers against a ten-man rush."

DeOssie could snap and recover in time to block. So when he was with Dallas, the Cowboys became the first team to split their ends away from the formation. Rather than everyone staying in tight, two players were split wide in a position that since has been known as the "gunners." The defense had to react and split players wide, as well.

"It became more of a premium if you could get a snapper to snap the ball accurately and block. Then, it certainly takes a lot of pressure off your punt protection and it helps your punt coverage," the coach explained. "When you have to bring those guys in tight, and then they jam at the line of scrimmage and then you get nobody down there … that was a big change in the game, and that was in the mid '80s.

"He was the first one that really allowed teams to do that. People copied it, and then other snappers came along. Guys like the Todd Christensens of the world, who were regular players and good snappers, were ultimately replaced by the specialists.

"Of course, as the rosters expanded, then that made it easier to be able to afford to carry a snapper, and also returners, all the specialists," Belichick concluded.

Belichick not only does all the coaching; he is also one of only a handful of men in the last twenty years who have served as general manager. He has his hands on everything, literally everything, involving his team. That, of course, is a change for Robert Kraft, the owner. Bill Parcells was not given the same leeway.

"They want you to cook the dinner, at least they should let you shop for the groceries," is the way he described it at one of his press conferences.

Many likely do not realize that the Pats long have had one of the smallest coaching staffs in the league. In 2014, for example, they had eighteen. Only the Steelers, with seventeen, and the Panthers, with sixteen, had fewer. Several staffs had twenty-five coaches.

The sad part is that Belichick's legacy will forever be tarnished because of the brushes with the rules his team has had, from Spygate to Deflategate. He is a great coach. But his personality and his willingness to push rules to the limit have hit home. Early in 2015, when more than one national pundit wrote about how the Patriots' reputation has been permanently tarnished, Belichick addressed the situation more directly than he ever had.

"I just think overall, it's kind of sad, really, to see some stories written that obviously have an agenda to them with misinformation and anonymous-type comments," he said. "Writing about warm drinks and trash cans and stuff like that, it's just a sad commentary, and it's gone to a pretty low level. It's sunk pretty deep.

"First of all, I would say that I think our program here is built on competition and trying to improve every day and trying to work hard, and it's not built on excuses," he went on. "And we just try to go to work and improve and find a way to get better. This organization has won a lot of games, but particularly in reference to the great teams from '01, '03, '04, and all the great players that played on those teams: Ty Law, (Lawyer) Milloy, Otis Smith, Rodney Harrison, (Tedy) Bruschi, (Larry) Izzo, (Willie) McGinest, (Mike) Vrabel, (Anthony) Pleasant, (Richard) Seymour, Matt Light, (Joe) Andruzzi, Steve Neal, (Deion) Brnach, Troy Brown, (Tom) Brady, Antowain Smith, Kevin Faulk, Corey Dillon,

Lonie Paxton, (Adam) Vinatieri—to take away what those guys accomplished, what those teams accomplished, how good they were, how many great players we had, how well they played in big games, how they consistently showed up and made big plays and game-winning plays, it's just not right.

"Those guys were great players. And many more. Those were a few of them and great teams," he said. "So I'm not going to get into a back and forth on it, but that's the way I feel about it."

Unfortunately, he is correct there, too. It is unfair to the players who accomplished so much. But the atmosphere Belichick created and fostered is the reason why. He did it to himself.

What made Belichick's surly, I-wish-I didn't-have-to-do-this attitude that much more difficult for those of us who had to work with him every day was that he followed two others who were on the opposite extreme.

Bill Parcells and Pete Carroll were a reporter's dream, two guys who all but did your work for you. Unlike Belichick, who feels that providing any information before a game is merely aiding the enemy, Parcells and Carroll knew that helping promote the game was part of their job. And they were both very good at it. They did not need a Berj Najarian to prepare them. Their systems somehow managed to win Super Bowls, too.

Parcells was an absolute showman, perfect for the New York and Boston markets. You almost did not need to ask questions; simply point him in the direction of the topic of the game, and he took off. Newspaper guys, radio people, television personalities, it did not matter. Parcells made everyone look good.

One of the more memorable interviews I ever had was with Parcells soon after he took the New England head-coaching job in 1993. By then, Parcells had already won two Super Bowls and established himself as one of the biggest names in the coaching game. Everyone knew all about him—or so it seemed.

As always happens when a new guy comes in, everyone wanted a private interview to gather information and do a feature on him. The networks and major-market television stations and newspapers all got their one-on-ones with Parcells. Because Providence and Hartford were one rung down on the priority list—the Triple-A teams, rather than the big leagues, if you will—we were told that we would get a two-on-one. We could have Parcells for twenty minutes, but we would have to do it together. So, Terry Price, the *Hartford Courant's* beat writer, and I sat at a small table in one of the meeting rooms, and Parcells arrived right on time.

From the first question, Parcells was outstanding. He was open and enthusiastic and, most of all, tremendously helpful. He knew that we were looking for information that might not be as well known. He took us in all kinds of directions, from his days growing up in New Jersey, to his love of the Red Sox, to his coaching philosophy and even to his love of horses and horse racing. He was already in the horse-race business by that time.

The end result was that I wrote one of the longest one-subject stories of my career. There was just too much good information to pass up. The interview went well past the planned twenty minutes, but Parcells did not look at the clock. No one came in to tell him he had to go. He let Terry and I exhaust everything we had, and he openly responded to everything.

Not that the interview was the exception. He was like that almost every day. His personality was ideal to deal with the media. Fans got to see more of his personality when he went into television after he retired from coaching. He was good. But television, with its restricted time frame, did not let the full Parcells come out. He was at his best when there was no time limit and he could tell story after story about his fabled career.

When he left after his famous falling out with Robert Kraft, the team owner—Parcells did have a very big ego, to be sure—Carroll stepped in, and the "degree of difficulty" meter for the media barely moved.

CHAPTER 3

TOM BRADY

The Tom Brady who came to New England in 2000 was very different than the Tom Brady who now is rewriting the NFL record book.

The quarterback arrived with no fanfare. He had fallen to the sixth round in the draft, the 199th player selected, because scouts felt he had physical issues that would make it difficult for him to compete in the NFL. The various scouting reports that have since been made public had a list of negatives.

"Lacks great physical stature and strength," one read. "Frame not big enough, not strong," reported another. Brady had done very poorly in the annual Scouting Combine. The fastest time he ran in the forty-meter was 5.14, which is a little below average. Most of his other times were worse, up to the high six seconds, which is poor even for an offensive lineman. His other measurable, such as ninety-nine inches in the broad jump, a vertical leap of 24.5 inches, were not those of a high draft choice.

Another scouting report summed up his situation: "Does everything slowly."

Still, Brady had been productive in the last two of his five years at Michigan. He had just led the Wolverines to a come-from-behind victory over Alabama in the Orange Bowl. He had one fan in Dick Rehbein, the Patriots quarterback coach, who had personally scouted Brady. It was Rehbein, Bill Belichick has said, who was the biggest booster pushing Brady's selection.

Shortly after he arrived in Foxboro, Shane Donaldson was one of the first to learn about some of the positives this new guy had. At the time, he was the fourth quarterback on the roster, someone who many of us thought was simply hoping to make the practice squad. Donaldson had just graduated from URI and was hired by *Patriots Football Weekly*. One of his first assignments was to write a weekly diary with one of the rookies, which would focus on how a player makes the transition from college to the pros.

The player selected was Tom Brady.

"He kind of spoiled me," Donaldson said of the experience. "He was so good to work with, so smart, so helpful. He made it easy. I thought everybody would be like him."

Brady took the job seriously. He was open and very helpful. It brought up some of the positives that scouts had listed in their reports. They had called him, "very poised and composed, smart and alert, can read coverages, good accuracy and touch." Oh, yes, Brady also had the highest score of anyone the Patriots drafted that year on the Wonderlic Test, the standardized psychological exam all prospects take at the Draft Combine.

As everyone knows, Brady made the team as a rookie and watched Drew Bledsoe guide the Patriots. The next season, Brady had worked his way up to the number-two spot on the depth chart. After the Patriots began the season 0–2, Bledsoe was injured when he took a crushing hit by the Jets Mo Lewis.

During training camp that year, the forty-five-year-old Rehbein had been stricken with a heart attack while exercising and died. It was decided that the team would not hire a replacement, that Belichick would add helping coach the quarterbacks to his already long list of duties. After Brady had led the Patriots to an 11–3 record in the final fourteen games to earn a spot in the playoffs, the subject of helping coach the quarterbacks came up before the divisional championship game against Oakland. The memorable game would become known as the Snow Bowl, the one in which an obscure rule called "the tuck rule" allowed the Patriots to win a game they appeared to have lost. That and a fabulous field goal in the snow by Adam Vinatieri made the difference.

As great as that game was, an interview two days before the game was special for me. It told me a lot about Brady.

Belichick had downplayed his role as quarterback coach in a press conference before the game.

"We've been doing that all year. I try not to screw him up," the coach said.

Later, in the locker room, I was speaking with Dan Pires of the *New Bedford Standard Times,* and we both mentioned that we had not realized the quarterback coaching situation. We thought it warranted more investigation because Brady was, for all practical purposes, a rookie.

21

Dan and I headed to the far side of the locker room where the quarterbacks had their locker in old Foxboro Stadium. Brady was alone. When we told him what we wanted to ask him about, he brightened. He clearly was happy to talk about it. It turned into one of the best interviews I ever had with the Patriots.

Brady spoke about how Belichick was coaching him unlike anyone else ever had. He did not deal with mechanics and techniques at all. Rather, the focus was explaining why and how defenses try to make life difficult for a quarterback. Belichick, of course, built his reputation as the defensive coordinator with the Giants under Bill Parcells.

"When you are around him, you learn," Brady began. "I'll say, 'Well, Coach, why did they do this?' And he'll say, 'If I was the defensive coordinator, this is what I would be doing.' It's pretty neat to get that type of input. Normally, you do not get that type of insight.

"'Coach, why did they play this coverage?'" Brady went on. "'Well, this is their run blitz. Or, 'This is their pass blitz.' Or, 'This is what their defensive coordinator is like. This is what their defensive coordinator has done for the last twelve years.' That stuff. It helps a lot.'

"He does seem to like it. It helps us a lot, because he really understands the defense," he said. "He really understands what they're trying to do." A bit earlier, Belichick had explained why he decided to be the quarterback coach for that one year.

"I think it's important, both philosophically and from a game-management standpoint, that the coach and quarterback are on the same page," Belichick said. "We talk regularly during the week about what's going to happen, how we're doing it, and then we review what did happen. Then we move on to the next stage."

It was merely one example of how Brady wanted to learn and used knowledge to make himself a better player. It is a trait he has not only maintained, but built on through the years. Mix that in with the fact that he worked just as hard on strengthening the physical weaknesses that had scared away the scouts, and he'd made himself into a new man.

Brady provided a detailed explanation of his physical work in an interview with Bodybuilding.com in 2012. He spoke about how he works out every Monday, Tuesday, Thursday, and Friday with weights, does forty to sixty minutes of cardio six days a week, and, to improve his mobility, does drills involving shuffling, sliding, and jump roping. That is coupled with taking regular vitamins, following a strict diet, and eating natural foods.

Away from football, one aspect of Brady's personality that I feel helped him deal with becoming a household name is that he likes the spotlight. He has never shied away from celebrity. In fact, it is just the opposite.

Many of the Patriots players live in the small towns around the stadium. Some live in Rhode Island, where several condo developments make places available for Patriots players at good prices. Brady lived in Boston from day one. He wanted to be in the big city, be where the notoriety is. He was never listed in the gossip columns as dating a waitress or a clerk in a department store. The mother of his first child is an actress. His wife and mother of his two youngest children is one of the most famous, and highest paid, models in the world.

His accomplishments are mind-boggling. He has set records with a twenty-one-game winning streak, the most consecutive passes without an interception (358), and fifty touchdown passes in one season. He and Belichick have won more games as a team than any coach/quarterback combination in league history. All this is on top of his four Super Bowl titles and six appearances in the title game.

In NFL history, there have been only four late-round draft choices (sixth round or later) that made it to the Hall of Fame. They are Shannon Sharpe, taken in the seventh round by the Broncos out of Savannah State in 1990; Rayfield Wright, selected by the Cowboys in the seventh round in 1967 out of Fort Valley State; Richard Dent, taken by the Bears in the eighth round in 1983; and Ken Houston, Houston's ninth-round pick in 1969.

Two others who were never drafted, Antonio Gates, the former basketball player at Kent State, and Adam Vinatieri, the kicker from South Dakota State, could be added to that list. Brady is a lock to join that club, too.

In working with Brady and Belichick, I was convinced that the two were a perfect match. Belichick is best known for his ability as a game-day coach. He draws up different game plans for every opponent and reacts to situations on the field as they happen as well as anyone. His teams always get better as the season goes along, to the point of dominating by December.

New England fans like to debate who is more responsible for the dynasty the team has put together, Brady or Belichick. From where I sat, it was not even close. Belichick is by far the biggest reason the team has been so successful. If Brady had arrived under a different coach, it is highly doubtful the team would have come even close to compiling the records it has since 2000.

That being said, Belichick needed someone like Brady to carry out his plan, someone as bright, as intense, and as hard-working as Brady. There are very few athletes who have taken their job more seriously and worked at it any harder than Tom Brady has. He is the model any athlete in any sport could use to show the right way to go about building a career. He also is the shining example of how good a player could become by working hard and learning from Belichick.

CHAPTER 4

THE RED SOX

As with so many others who grew up in New England in the post-World War II era, baseball was my first love. It was the game of choice any time we had free time and the weather permitted. We were always outside. No one stayed in the house looking at television or a computer.

We would play in the vacant lot next to Richard Fleury's house. We would play at Jerry Viens's because he had the biggest yard in the neighborhood. When we could not round up enough kids to play a game, I'd have a game of catch with Bobby Nolette or Rene Leveillee, who were my two closest neighbors on West Warwick's West Street.

The big treat would be when my father, George, would arrange a trip to Boston to see the Red Sox. Three or four times a year, we would get in the '57 Ford station wagon, head up the back roads through Coventry, Scituate, and Smithfield for a half hour to his brother Harold's house in North Smithfield, and pick up my uncle and my cousin, Chuck. Then it would be another hour or so up Route One to Fenway. It was one of the highlights every year.

Ted Williams, Bill Monboquette, and Billy Goodman, our first sports heroes, helped draw us in. And so did Curt Gowdy and Ned Martin.

Gowdy and Martin were the radio broadcasters. It was a nightly ritual to place the transistor radio on the stand next to the bed and listen as we went to sleep. The next day, we would read stories about the tremendous accomplishments by Williams or the escapades of Jimmy Pearsall or the pitching of Dick Radatz. We would cringe when Gowdy described how Don Buddin made another error or Frank Malzone another diving play at third base.

We had one glorious year when Yaz carried the Sox to an Impossible Dream in 1967, and another in 1975 when Pudge Fisk and the Sox "won" the Series three games to four against the Big Red Machine. Every year, though, ended the same way '75 did, with more frustration and the idea that the Sox might never win a title.

Even after I married and got a job working for a newspaper, the fever never went away. I drew my family into it. I talked Pauline into planning our annual family vacation around baseball. We would take whatever time we had, from four days to a week, drive to a Major League city, and do three things: see a game, tour the city, and visit an amusement park. It was part educational for the kids and great fun for all of us.

We did it for eight years, until the boys (John is almost four years older than Jayson) got old enough that they did not want to spend their time with their parents anymore. We drove to New York twice (both sons liked Yankee Stadium better than Shea). We went to Baltimore, where we tied it in with a visit to the White House. We went to Philadelphia, where we took pictures of the kids touching the Liberty Bell; to Toronto, where the CN Tower and city made a hugely positive impression; and to Montreal, where we ran into M. Charles Bakst, then the *Journal*'s lead political writer, while we were at the Expos game.

The last year we did it, we flew to San Diego and saw Fernando Valenzuela shut out the Padres. Five days later, we were supposed to see Valenzuela pitch again in Chavez Ravine. We spent the day at Knottsberry Farm amid light rain. We left early to get to the game and heard on the radio it had been postponed.

It was not a disaster. We had another day in LA. The next day, our last on the trip, we took in Disneyland, again with light rain, but left early to get to the game. As we were driving, we heard the announcement that the game was postponed. I believe it is, to this day, the only time the Dodgers ever have had two straight home games rained out.

We have great memories of all the trips. There are pictures of the family at the Statue of Liberty, at the Empire State Building, and at the San Diego Zoo. One of my treasured possessions is a small picture taken as John, Jay, and I were going down the flume ride at Six Flags New Jersey, part of one of the New York trips. John is nine and laughing wildly as our log flies down the big hill toward the water. Jayson, at age five, is not thrilled. He has a look of horror. For me, it shows off a full head of hair, which was soon to disappear. I keep the tiny picture on my bureau as a memory of a wonderful trip.

Baseball was an integral part of our lives, so it is not hard to guess what my reaction was in May of 1991, when I was told my assignment was being changed. I would do baseball full-time.

29

The *Journal* always had excellent baseball coverage. From Harold Rich and Joe McEnry when I was growing up, to Art Turgeon when I began at the paper, and then to Sean McAdam and Steven Krasner in the 1980s and '90s, the Red Sox writers all were total pros. I had been switched from covering high schools to doing college basketball in 1989 and had helped out with an occasional Red Sox or Patriots assignment at that point. I was forty-three years old, no longer a kid by any means. I'd like to say I was a sophisticated pro by then. But I have to admit, I was excited at the chance to work at Fenway Park and at the opportunity to meet and work with the Red Sox.

As with anything else, I learned very quickly that reality is not like fantasy. It was a job like any other job, and not necessarily the most pleasant one.

This was the era when the atmosphere in the Red Sox clubhouse was strained at times with the media. Players like Roger Clemens and Nomar Garciaparra did not always deal well with reporters. I could understand part of it. When players arrived at the park, reporters were already there, waiting to talk to them, often even as they were dressing. There were times when Garciaparra would get upset because there were so many people in the way, he had trouble even getting to his locker. I was there the day a red line appeared in the locker room in front of each locker, a line the reporters were told they were not allowed to cross. I was not there the day Clemens became so upset with something written about him that he got into an argument with the writer, a shouting match that ended when Clemens took a hot dog from the grill, threw it at the writer, and yelled, "Have another hot dog, you fat pig."

Clemens, in particular, interested me because of my fascination with how and why people act the way they do. He was like two different people: the guy on the field, who was one of the best of his generation, and the one off the field, who thought the world had to submit to him because he was such a great player.

Clemens turned out to be one of the truly unusual people I ever worked with. Here are two incidents that left me shaking my head about the way the off-field Clemens acted.

One came when the Red Sox were in Minnesota for a three-game midweek series. As it happens so often, all three games were at night, which meant the players had to find something to do for the first half of the day. For a good chunk of this team, that meant finding a good golf course to enjoy.

Clemens is a serious golfer. So are Frank Viola, Greg Harris, and Tom Brunansky, among others. Bob Montgomery, one of the team's broadcasters, is the best golfer of all and often helped arrange outings.

On this day, there were two groups of Sox players and one made up of media members who made the quick trip to Chaska. The course was Hazeltine, one of the special Robert Trent Jones designs. Just a year earlier, the course had hosted the US Open. Even by Red Sox standards, this was a special outing. Bob Starr, the Red Sox broadcaster, and George Kimball, a *Boston Herald* columnist who loved golf, were part of our group.

As we gathered in the pro shop, one of the young assistant pros welcomed us and spoke about how the day would be a bit different because Hazeltine officials required that a member play with each group. Oh, yes, he added, the fee for the day would be fifty dollars, including carts.

That raised eyebrows. The Red Sox were not accustomed to having to pay to play. Almost everywhere they went, they were welcome visitors who were full guests for the day. They did not have to pay. There might have been some minor grumbling when the young pro told them of Hazeltine rules, but almost everyone dug into his pocket and paid. There was one exception.

Clemens did not. When the young pro realized he was one short, he sought out Clemens and asked for the fee. Clemens looked at him and said, "I'm Roger Clemens."

"Yes, I know, Mr. Clemens," the pro said. "I just have to get the fee from everyone."

"You don't understand. I'm Roger Clemens," the pitcher shot back.

After a few uneasy seconds, Viola stepped in and pulled Clemens away. He said he wanted to show Clemens this nice set of clubs he had seen. Brunansky pulled the pro aside, gave him the money, and said, "We're all set now, right?"

The pro said yes, everything was settled, and soon, everyone was out playing the Open course.

Later in the same season, the Sox were at home, and when we returned to the clubhouse after batting practice, Clemens was at his locker speaking with Billy Andrade. Andrade was a PGA Tour player from Rhode Island who I had been covering since he was a teenager. I walked over to say hi. They were talking about golf—Clemens had been Andrade's partner in the PGA Tour event at Pebble Beach. We talked golf for about seven or eight minutes. It could not have been more pleasant. Clemens was great. When it broke up, Clemens pleasantly wished us well, Billy went out to get ready for the game, and I went about doing my job.

The next day, I tried to use the incident to help me with my work. Clemens always had been difficult to speak to, especially for those of us who were not the big hitters on the media beat. I thought that since we had such a pleasant conversation the previous night, I would say hello again, make sure he remembered who I was, and hope it would help me in the future.

I went to Clemens when he seemed to have a free moment and asked him some sort of golf question. He looked at me, never said a word, and turned away. It was as if the previous night had never happened.

What made actions like that difficult to understand was that the Roger Clemens who took the pitcher's mound was so good. He was a maniacal competitor, which added to his tremendous talent. It was impossible not to have total respect for Clemens as a pitcher, as a winner. He was one of the fiercest competitors I ever saw in any sport. On the field, he was special. But off the field, I thought he was as big a blockhead as I've ever worked with.

As I learned, what a writer had to do was compensate. If there were guys tough to deal with, you sought out others who were not. Tony Pena became one of my go-to guys. He was terrific. Kenny Ryan, a relief pitcher who had grown up in Seekonk, Massachusetts, was excellent. Viola, Brunansky, Eric Wedge, Luis Rivera, Tony Fossas, and Jody Reed all helped me do my job. A young Mo Vaughn came up to begin what would be an excellent career. He also would help change the atmosphere in the clubhouse for the better as far as I was concerned.

The manager helped smooth matters over between the media and the team in my first year. That was Joe Morgan, the baseball lifer who grew up near Fenway and was one of the most affable people in the world.

33

Also, it helped to be able to make contacts off the field. Dick Bresciani, the Red Sox vice president of public affairs, was a big help. Rhode Island's Lou Gorman, a baseball lifer and a front office executive for many years, was a terrific resource and was happy to chat anytime, anywhere. In later years, Jeremy Kapstein, another Rhode Islander who was among baseball's first agents, later CEO of the Padres and senior advisor with the Red Sox, became a good friend and mentor. There were still plenty of positives with the job.

Still, it was something of a culture shock. For the twenty years or so that I covered the Red Sox, most of that part-time, the atmosphere in Boston was different than the one in New York. The Yankees, obviously, are the big rivals that Sox fans do not like. But my attitude changed when working with the two teams was my job. While the Sox could be difficult, the Yankees were dominated by pleasant personalities like Derek Jeter, Bernie Williams, Mariano Rivera, and Paul O'Neill. They were great to work with. The fact that Joe Torre, one of the ultimate good guys, was the manager, made the Yanks that much easier to like and respect.

The Red Sox situation was much better by 2004, when the "Cowboy Up" team won the World Series and ended eighty-six years of frustration. David Ortiz, Pedro Martinez, Johnny Damon, Kevin Millar, Jason Varitek, and manager Terry Francona, among others, were much easier to work with. I did not cover the 2004 playoffs when Curt Schilling, Ortiz, and friends helped change baseball history in Boston. I must say, sitting at home and watching brought back the old feelings of openly rooting for the Sox. It was wonderful, topped by an unprecedented rally from three games down against the Yankees.

Professionally, I was disappointed that I did not have the chance to cover what was one of the greatest sports stories of my lifetime. But in some ways, I was happy I was not working those playoffs. I was able to enjoy them with everyone else in New England. And boy, did we ever enjoy it.

The good feelings have carried over. The arrival of Dustin Pedroia, one of the great guys to work with, was part of a large group of home-produced players who made work at Fenway more pleasant than it had been. Francona was in the class of Bill Parcells as someone who understood the process and who knew everyone had a job to do, so he tried to help. He went out of his way to be fair and reasonable with everyone. He is a truly good man.

Regardless of the personalities involved, I learned that the reality is that covering baseball is the most demanding job a sportswriter can have. With games played almost every day, there is no letdown. For us at the *Journal,* a typical workday for home games was eleven or twelve hours. We had to leave early enough to make the one-hour drive to Boston in time for the manager's daily meeting at 3:30. At times, we had to be there even earlier if we had to chase players for interviews. The best way to get the players was while they were getting dressed so as to get out of their way before they began their work in the weight room or on the field.

The trip in for the games turned into an instructional period for me. Leo Labossiere, an old friend from my days covering high school sports and the former athletic director at Central Falls High, was a scout, first for the White Sox and later for the Orioles, where his boss was fellow Central Falls native Roland Hemond. Leo was older at the time and did not like to drive at night. I was happy to pick him up and drive him in. He became a constant instructor for me on the game's inner workings, as well as a source who provided me with helpful information about players. Leo would compile his reports while I wrote my stories after the game. As we drove home, I would pick his brain for more helpful information about individual players.

During the first year I covered baseball, 1991, it was a thrill to do road games. To go inside Yankee Stadium and walk on the field was a kick. To sit in the press box in old Tiger Stadium in Detroit and have to worry about getting hit by foul balls because we were so close to the field was a novelty. To drive up almost to the front door in Kansas City, where the closest parking was reserved for the media, and walk straight in to Kauffman Stadium, cover the game, and then head to Arthur Bryant's for BBQ was, well, it was a great way to spend time.

But the job meant too much time away from home. My boys were growing, and I was missing many of their games, not to mention catching up with whatever they were doing. I called home one night from Chicago, and Jayson picked up the phone excitedly. He had hit his first home run in Little League play the previous night. He was thrilled. I was upset I was not there to see it.

For better or worse, I have always been a homebody. There were many times after games, both home and away, when the writers would go out for a beer or two. I was one of the wallflowers who would say no thanks and head home or back to the hotel. The combination of the travel, the long hours, and not being able to see some of the important moments as my sons grew got to me. After two years of being a card-carrying member of the Baseball Writers Association of America, I went to my editors and asked if I could go back to my old job of being the office utility guy. I was thrilled when they agreed to it.

It ended up being the ideal situation for me. I still covered ten to twenty games at Fenway each year, and about that many with the Triple-A team at Pawtucket. I got to go back to golf and college basketball, my first loves, help with football, and be on call for anything else that came up. Doing a little bit of everything was what I most enjoyed.

CHAPTER 5

THE PAWSOX

For Pawtucket Red Sox players, the goal is to make their time in McCoy Stadium merely a stepping-stone. Fenway Park is where they want to be. They want McCoy to be their final stop on the climb to the Major Leagues. Over the last forty years, about five hundred guys who have played at McCoy have gone on to the big leagues.

At a certain point in my career, I started hoping to go the other way. As I got older, I much preferred McCoy over Fenway.

Obviously, it was not that way at the beginning. Some of my best memories were the trips to Fenway. I remember seeing Ted Williams play. I remember a number of times getting seats in the right-field stands when the Tigers were in town. We would head over to the visiting bullpen at some point during the game, and my father would chat with Mike Roarke, the Tigers' back-up catcher. People would look over and wonder why we were talking to one of the players. Roarke was from West Warwick, too. He knew my father, who worked in the post office and knew everyone in town.

The entire experience was thrilling, including stopping at the old Beau May diner in Woonsocket for a hamburger and french fries on the way home. Fenway was, and is, truly a special place. But the difficulty in dealing with some of the players, and the long hours required for doing the job, burned away much of the luster. It took awhile, but somewhere along the line, I let our sports editors, first Dave Bloss and later Art Martone, know that I would be happy to go to Pawtucket rather than Boston.

I understood that I was being unusual. Most reporters beg for the chance to be in the bigs, just as the players do. Everything is bigger and more important. The recognition that comes along with being a member of the Baseball Writers of America feels good. Our two prime baseball writers at the time, Sean McAdam and Steve Krasner, both would lobby to do Boston as often as possible rather than getting "demoted" to Pawtucket when help was needed there. It was normal to want to be part of the Major League scene.

The situation in Pawtucket helped change that, at least for me. For me, it was a lot more fun seeking out Josh Reddick or Dustin Pedrioa or David Murphy or any of a hundred others and speaking with them one on one. In Boston, there were so many reporters squeezed into the tiny clubhouse that it was difficult to speak with players one on one.

In Pawtucket, it was a way of life. Rather than forty, fifty, or sixty people trying to work, on a typical day, there would be two or three at McCoy. Brendan McGair was always there for the *Pawtucket Times,* my old paper. Many times, he would be the only other reporter around, although it was a lot more fun when Mike Scandura, who had retired from the *Times* and later worked for several Red Sox magazines, showed up. Mike is an unabashed Yankees fan, and he would take kidding all night, especially from Bruce Guindon, the official scorer.

As I got older, it also mattered that rather than an eleven or twelve-hour day in Boston, Pawtucket was a very normal eight-hour workday. In my later years, I had become a regular passenger rather than driver to Boston. Whenever possible, Joey McDonald, the terrific young reporter who had worked his way up from answering telephones to becoming a baseball writer, would chauffer me to Fenway. We would meet at 1:30 at the Cumberland Plaza and Joe would do all the work getting us to and from the park. It was a good night when we were back in Cumberland before one a.m.

Covering Pawtucket meant leaving home at three and usually getting back by eleven. Once at the park, of course, life was good with Ben Mondor, Bill Wanless, and the PawSox staff providing everything we needed to do our job.

The more informal atmosphere not only made it easier to work; it also helped provide material for stories. One of my favorite days happened on trade deadline day in 2008. The day is one of the most important of the year for a player in Triple-A. Many of the trades that are made involve dealing minor league prospects for aging veterans, so it can turn into a big break for a player.

On this day, the PawSox were going through their normal batting practice as the 4:00 p.m. deadline approached. George Kottaras, one of the catchers, was not playing that day. He was inside watching the big television in the clubhouse. I was curious what might happen, so I spent much of my time watching television rather than the work on the field.

NESN, the Sox television home, had a panel discussion going on relating the moves other teams had made. At almost exactly 4:00 p.m., the *Boston Globe's* Nick Cafardo walked off the set. He came back a couple minutes later and announced that he had learned that the Sox had made a trade with the Pirates. He said he did not have all the details yet, including who the Red Sox had obtained (it turned out to be Jason Bay, part of a bigger deal that also saw Manny Ramirez shipped to Los Angeles), but he did know that Brandon Moss of Pawtucket was involved.

Kottaras bolted up and ran out to the field. From the dugout, he pointed at Moss, put his thumb up, and waved it, as if to say, *You're outta here.* Moss saw what Kottaras was doing but did not understand. He put his glove out in front of him as if to say, *What are you talking about?*

At exactly the same time, manager Ron Johnson stopped throwing batting practice and stepped behind the mound. At the direction of Boston officials, he had taken his phone to the field and put it in his back pocket as he threw BP. He spoke for only a few seconds, waved to Rich Sauveur, the pitching coach, to take over for him, and began walking toward the dugout.

As he did, he pointed to Moss and waved at him to follow him inside. The other players saw all this happening and gave Moss a cheer as he headed in. Kottaras was roaring with laughter as Moss went past him and followed Johnson into the manager's office.

The two spent a couple minutes behind closed doors. When they emerged, Moss had something of a bemused smile, seemingly not sure what to make of what had just happened. Brendan McGair and I, the only reporters there, asked if we could speak to him.

"Just give me a minute, please," said Moss, who was one of the many pleasant guys to deal with on that team.

He went to his locker, took out his phone, and called his wife. They spent several minutes chatting before Moss sat down and waved us over to chat.

"That was my wife. I called to tell her, but she already knew. She was watching television. She knew I was traded before I did," Moss told us.

Later, Johnson met with us but said he did not have the details of the trade. All he knew was that he was losing Moss, one of his best players, but he was happy for Moss because he would be going to the big leagues. Working with the Pawtucket managers also was a bonus. The team had a run of excellent managers.

Johnson was one of the great guys to work with, a bundle of energy who was a reformed alcoholic. His son, Chris, used to regularly visit and work out with the team. Chris is now in the big leagues. Buddy Bailey, who was there before Johnson, Torey Lovullo, and Arnie Beyeler all helped make work pleasant by being so helpful and accommodating in the Pawtucket manager's office.

It also was fun to work with the players. Almost without exception, guys were happy to do interviews. They were still on the way up, and publicity almost always was positive. After getting to know the players, it was it was fun to see if their personality would change if they began making big money in the Major Leagues.

Ben Mondor in the owner's box at McCoy Stadium.

CHAPTER 6

BEN MONDOR

The first story I heard about Ben Mondor was not a good one.

It happened on the day he bought the Pawtucket Red Sox in 1977. I was still working at the *Pawtucket Times* at the time, and Ted Mulcahey, the sports editor, asked me to accompany him and do the straight news story.

The press conference, held at the old Howard Johnson's, was very normal. The team was in bankruptcy and had been a disaster for years. The new owner, a mill owner from Woonsocket, declared that he was going to make major changes. He was convinced the team could become both a benefit to the community and a profitable venture as well. It all sounded fine, but then again, it always does at this type of event.

I did my work, and the surprise came when I returned home that evening. Pauline asked what had happened. I told her I had spent the afternoon listening to a guy who had the same heavy French accent she has. Pauline grew up in Woonsocket.

"You might have heard of him. He's from Woonsocket," I told her. "Ben Mondor is his name."

She stopped what she was doing and exclaimed, "No, not him!"

"What do you mean?" I asked.

"I know him. He's mean," she responded.

She began explaining that several girls she knew worked in his office in a textile mill, many of which were still thriving in Woonsocket at the time. At least one of her friends quit because he was so difficult to work for.

Some years later, after everyone had learned that the mill-owning Mondor was very different than the baseball-team-owning Mondor, I told Ben the story. He responded with one of his big belly laughs as he shook his head in amusement.

"I guess my secret's out," he said when he gathered himself. "When you're in business, you have to do what you have to do."

Not only did he fail to deny the story; in some ways, he actually seemed proud of it. This Canadian immigrant, who grew up in a small community that no longer exists—it was flooded to make way for a reservoir—was a self-made man who was the living embodiment of the American dream. He turned the PawSox franchise into one of the best in the country.

The people who worked for him can testify about his hard-driving side. Almost to the end, they will tell you, he pushed them and demanded a lot. That was one of the secrets to his success. He sought out talented people who were good in their area of specialization and were hard workers themselves.

Mike Tamburro, the team CEO, was his first hire and stayed with him to the end. Lou Schwechheimer, the general manager, came on soon after as an intern and did not leave until after Mondor's death. Bill Wanless, who handled public relations, had opportunities to go to the big leagues, including with Boston, but stayed with Mondor. Mick Tedesco in stadium operations, Matt White the CFO, Michael Gwynn in marketing, Jim Hogan in concessions, Kevin Galligan in media creation, Jeff Bradley in communications, Goody Goodreau in the clubhouse—all of them were there ten, twenty, thirty years.

That stability might be the best testimony of all as to what type of franchise Mondor ran. People stayed because they were part of something good, something very good.

Yes, the owner worked hard and wanted everyone around him to work hard. But, as everyone who has been to McCoy Stadium in the last thirty-five years has learned, he had another side when it was time to relax. I would contend that by the time he died in 2010, he was the most beloved man in Rhode Island. And he deserved it.

The owner PawSox fans got to know and love acted like everyone's kindly grandfather with a heart of gold. He cleaned up every aspect of the organization, beginning with the stadium. Mondor had been blunt when someone asked what he thought of the then thirty-five-year-old facility built on a swamp.

"What a dump," he said.

Mondor did what he could to make McCoy presentable. But, with only a six thousand-seat capacity and major problems with the inner workings of the stadium, there was doubt as to whether it could continue. Many forget that in the late 1990s, there was talk that the team might move to Worcester because McCoy was in such poor shape.

The team, which leases the stadium from the city, announced in 1998 that it would renovate the facility to meet International League standards. The result was a $16 million project, jointly financed by the team and the state, which provided an extensive facelift that upped capacity to more than ten thousand, including a berm in left field where fans can sit on the grass, watch the action, and hope to catch home-run balls.

The inside work included new clubhouses for the teams that are better than some Major League teams have, including Boston's Fenway Park. The walkways inside the stadium feature great events in team history, from a visit by Ted Williams to display on The Longest Game, the thirty-three-inning affair in 1981 that began in April and ended in June.

The aspects that made Mondor and the franchise so well liked and respected had little to do with the physical surroundings. It was a place where the family could go and enjoy. Often, Mondor would be outside the stadium as fans arrived, would greet anyone and everyone, and simply did all he could to make everyone feel welcome.

Ticket prices were among the lowest in the International League through to the end of his ownership. In the thirty-four years he owned the team, he raised ticket prices only five times, for a total of four dollars. Concession prices remained stable for years. Parking was free. Everything was done right. The numbers tell the story of how fans reacted. The year before he bought the franchise, the team drew 70,354 fans. In 2005, the team drew 688,421 fans.

Beyond that, the team became a valued part of the community. Mondor did not look for recognition, but he donated to numerous charitable causes and established the Pawtucket Red Sox Charitable Foundation. Former PawSox and Red Sox manager Joe Morgan, who continued to be a regular visitor to McCoy long after he retired, once offered a simple but accurate description of Mondor: "He knows how to treat people," Morgan said. Among the many awards Mondor received was one of the highest honors bestowed by the state, the Distinguished Service Star, presented to him by Governor Lincoln Almond in 2002.

Mondor's courtesy extended to the team's managers, players, and reporters, too. Covering the PawSox was as pleasant an assignment as any all year. Players would tell stories about how, even after they had left Pawtucket, Mondor would keep in touch with them and their families.

Rhode Islanders sometimes have an inferiority complex because the state is so small and limited in what it can do. The history of how the state has handled major projects is filled with stories about waste and corruption. The story of the Pawtucket Red Sox under Ben Mondor was different. It was a genuine source of pride for the entire state.

CHAPTER 7

URI BASKETBALL

With apologies to Tom Wolfe, I am one of those who proved you can go home again—and love every minute of it.

In November 1989, my working life changed. After spending eleven very enjoyable years covering high school sports, I was transferred to the college and pro beat. I was hesitant at first, both because I was so happy doing what I was doing and because my first assignment would be covering University of Rhode Island basketball.

As a URI alum, I knew quite a bit about Rhody hoops. I was a regular at Keaney Gym in my years in school when Tom Carmody was the coach. I took a two-credit course, Coaching of Basketball, taught by Carmody and his assistant at the time, Lou Campanelli. In school, it was just something fun to do. As it turned out, it was a great help in my career. Carmody and Campanelli both were great people as well as excellent coaches and teachers. They taught me fundamentals that helped me for the next thirty years.

I told the editors of my background and my concern about whether I could do the work impartially. URI was a big part of my life. I loved my time there. It did everything for me a college is supposed to do.

The editors insisted they had no concerns, and besides, they said, I had dealt with much the same issue when I was working with the high schools. Hendricken, my old school, was the dominant athletic program in the state. I regularly had to deal with people criticizing me for writing too much about Hendricken. The truth was, though, that I was so conscious of the ties that Hendricken received less recognition than it deserved and, when it came to All-State selections, Hendricken athletes had to be above the crowd to receive the honor.

For better or worse, I took the same sensitivity to covering URI basketball. I learned very early on that there was no need for concern, at least in my mind. There were no decisions to make about which one of thirty or forty games played that night to write about, or how many players from one school to select for the All-State team. I was a reporter. I simply tried to tell everyone what happened at games, not comment on whether it was good or bad. In many ways, it was much simpler and easier work than trying to keep track of every high school in the state.

Plus, there was an added perk: traveling. We covered URI home and away, so I was able to see many parts of the country I had never seen before, all with the newspaper paying the tab. For someone who had not traveled much, it really was a major bonus.

My timing also was perfect because Al Skinner was in his second year as URI head coach. We will talk a lot about Skinner later, but we will begin with one of his coaching philosophies. That is, he loved to play in holiday tournaments, both to expose his players to those areas and to give his team more national visibility.

In the decade I worked with him, Skinner took URI to Hawaii, San Francisco, New Orleans, Arizona, El Paso, and Kansas City for holiday tournaments. Later, after he left, Jim Harrick and Jim Baron added places like Malibu and Las Vegas. All that, of course, was in addition to the regular trips taken every year to Philadelphia for the Atlantic-10 tournament and all the conference schools. It was a wonderful bonus, so much so that my wife joined me whenever she could, especially for the tournaments. We paid for her flight and meals, and the *Journal* paid for everything else. As I look back on it, I realize how fortunate I was to be in the right place at the right time to be able to do all these things. A generation earlier there were no such trips, or at least very few of them. These days, with the number of printed newspapers declining, stringers often are paid to cover an out-of-state event rather than having the beat reporter travel to the games. The people covering the teams these days are doing fewer away games every year.

What made the URI work even better was the fact that the people I had to work with were so good.

Skinner, a former University of Massachusetts star who had spent a decade playing pro ball, was beginning his second year as head coach. One of my first impressions was a bit disappointing. Jim Norman, the long-time sports information director at URI, told me I had better check with him before interviewing anyone because Al did not want some of his players to speak with reporters.

It was not a policy solely at URI. John Thompson, then one of the dominant coaches in the nation after building the Georgetown program into a power, was a leader in the trend. Freshmen were the ones prohibited from speaking. It was a measure designed to protect them. Skinner initiated the same policy for his team.

There was enough going on and I had so much to learn that it really wasn't a problem. I dug into the job, which quickly revived my love of college basketball. I found Skinner easy to work with and always available for interviews when I needed him. Actually, he was more than easy to work with. He was terrific to work with.

Somewhere in the middle of the season, Jim Norman mentioned, as we were getting ready for a game, that I could talk to anyone I wanted. He did not know why. He said Skinner had just told him to forward the information to me. Soon after, I asked Skinner what had changed.

He said something to the effect of, "I've seen enough on how you do your job. I trust you. I know you will be fair. I know you won't embarrass anyone."

It meant a lot to me. It also was the start of what turned out to be one of the strongest relationships I ever built with anyone I covered. Skinner proved to be not only an excellent coach who later went on to win more games at Boston College than any coach in Eagle history, but also an honest and straightforward person to deal with.

Unlike so many others in the coaching fraternity, Skinner is a quiet, somewhat introverted guy. It took a while, but as the years went along, he opened up about his background and why he acted the way he did. He spoke openly about how basketball saved his life, even made his life. Growing up in Long Island, he had no idea what he wanted to do. It was basketball that provided him guidance and a route to a good living. He wanted to do the same for as many youngsters as he could. He could relate to his players because he had grown up the same way many of them had.

Skinner's staff also was a huge help. He had hired Tim O'Shea, an outstanding, personable former BC player, and Bill Coen, a gentlemanly, bright guy who had played Division III basketball at Hamilton College, as his top assistants. They both went on to become successful head coaches in their own right and are still coaching today.

There was a division of labor, with the head coach overseeing everything, O'Shea working with the offense, and Coen with the defense. In those days, reporters not only covered the away games; they often traveled with the team, something that's no longer done today. Jim Norman, the sports information director, would give me the travel schedule, including flight times, hotels where the team would be staying, and the cost of everything. I would go over it with my editors, and we would give Norman the list of when we wanted to travel and/or stay with the team. The *Journal* would then pay URI.

It meant that I often stayed in the same hotel and found myself spending time in the lobby or hotel restaurant, or even the hotel bar, with the coaches. Skinner kept to himself and rarely was seen around the hotel. Coen and O'Shea, on the other hand, became my tutors. I bugged them whenever I had the opportunity about strategy questions, about how they went about their work recruiting players and anything and everything involving Division I basketball. They were a huge help.

Among the stories they told were many about how good a person Skinner was. They spoke about how genuine he was about wanting good kids who would represent the school in the right way on his team. Whenever there were problems, they spoke about how

Skinner would deal with them. On most teams, they said, the head coach had so many things to do that he would delegate others to deal with non-basketball issues. Skinner would deal with them himself.

Another benefit of travelling with the team was that I got to know the players pretty well. There was a long list of terrific young men who played for the Rams in that era. There are so many I hesitate to name any, but guys like Preston Murphy, Ibn Bakari, Carlos Cofield, Andre Samuel, Josh King, Parfait Bitee, Keith Cothran, Lamont Ulmer, and Will Martell come to mind. The team's two broadcasters, Steve McDonald and Don Kaull, were excellent to work with and quite often of much assistance in helping me do my job. They remain good friends of mine to this day.

The team had its ups and downs from season to season but always represented the school well. It was building to a peak when Skinner left URI for Boston College. The stability the program had under Skinner soon was only a memory.

CHAPTER 8

THE RYAN CENTER

Before Al Skinner left URI, he made perhaps the biggest contribution any coach ever has made at the school. He did it with the help of URI grads Lincoln Almond and Tom Ryan.

The URI basketball team's home from 1953 to 2002 was Keaney Gym. It was a great facility for its time, but by the end of the twentieth century, the 3,200-seat facility simply was not good enough for a basketball program hoping to keep up with its Division I competitors.

Basketball coaches and boosters at the school had been seeking a new, bigger facility for some time. It was Skinner who spearheaded the movement that got it done.

I state those facts because there are some, even at URI, who think Jim Harrick, the man who succeeded Skinner, was the one who deserves the credit. It is an understandable misconception since Skinner left for BC before the building was finished. Harrick certainly did help, primarily with his coaching, which guided the Rams to the Elite Eight in 1998 using the players Skinner left behind. Harrick's on-court success helped bring in donations as the fundraising campaign was at its high point. It also helped create good feelings at the State House with the legislators who had to approve the project.

The fact is, though, that nothing would have happened without Skinner doing all the legwork.

In his typically quiet style, he went behind the scenes and pleaded his cause. In the 1990s, when Rhode Island had a Republican governor in Lincoln Almond, he received the boost he needed. Almond was the first URI grad ever elected governor. He also is a basketball fan who still attends Rhody games to this day. Almond took up the cause behind the scenes. Working with Skinner, the two received the support they needed—provided, that is, that enough money could be raised for what turned out to be a $54 million project.

That's when Ryan, a URI pharmacy grad, helped make it all possible. By this time, the New Jersey native had risen from a pharmacist in a CVS Pharmacy in Woonsocket to CEO of the company, now listed in the Fortune 100.

Ryan gave the campaign a great boost when he and his wife, Kathy, donated $5 million, which led to the facility being named in his honor.

Getting the go-ahead was one thing. The last hurdle was getting a building that would suit the school and the team. Athletic director Ron Petro did not delegate the assignment. He took personal responsibility for making plans. The HOK Corporation, one of the famed architectural companies in the world, was hired to do the design.

Petro was a former basketball player and coach, so he knew what was needed. He visited other college campuses to pick up ideas and suggestions on how to go about putting together the building. He received proposals to have the facility seat anywhere from six thousand to twelve thousand fans.

The project will go down as Petro's greatest contribution to the school. He and the HOK architects settled on a 7,687-seat arena, ideal for URI. All seats are in a rectangular octagon and within eighty-four feet of the court. The exterior is classic Rhode Island with panels representing lighthouses on three sides. Rhode Islanders long have been accustomed to seeing major projects bungled. But the entire Ryan Center campaign went beautifully, and the facility today is one of the best in the Atlantic 10.

The first men's game in the new building, on November 22, 2002, was a classic. Henry Bibby had agreed to bring his Southern Cal team in to christen the building. The game was tied at seventy-one when URI's Dustin Hellenga made a fadeaway jumper from the left baseline with 2.2 seconds left to put URI ahead. While URI began to celebrate, the Trojans threw the ball long to Desmon Farmer on the left wing. His three-pointer bounced off the rim twice and dropped through. Bibby and the Trojans ran off the court celebrating a victory.

About ten minutes later, they found out they'd lost. Officials went to television replays, which were not quite as efficient then as they are now. Their job was made more difficult because the shot came as the buzzer was sounding. After considerable study, the officials ruled the shot came too late and URI had the victory. Bibby later called it the worst officiated game he had ever seen.

Linda Bruno, the commissioner of the Atlantic 10, present
Bob Vetrano Award to Paul and Pauline Kenyon

CHAPTER 9
THE JIMS, HARRICK AND BARON

Al Skinner's departure brought about big changes in the URI basketball program.

It had taken Skinner some time to settle in as a head coach, but once he did, the program became a strong one. His teams played in two NCAA and two NIT tournaments in his last six seasons. It was peaking when he left in 1997 after compiling a 12–4 Atlantic 10 record, 20–10 overall, and played in the NCAA Tournament. He had players like Tyson Wheeler, Cuttino Mobley, Antonio Reynolds-Dean, Preston Murphy, and Luther Clay returning. There was every reason to believe the team would be even better the next year.

Skinner's move to Boston College, brought on in part because he and athletic director Ron Petro had trouble agreeing on a contract, threatened to set everything back. A surprise choice to replace him kept everything going forward, at least in the short run.

One of URI's biggest boosters, Bob Terino, a URI grad who owned a jewelry-making business, first suggested and then actively campaigned for a guy who two years before had won the national championship: Jim Harrick.

Harrick was the second-winningest coach in UCLA history, after the legendary John Wooden. However, he was caught in scandal over providing improper benefits to his players shortly after winning the national championship. That would have been a relatively minor issue, but Harrick lied in attempting to cover it up. Then he tried to get others to lie for him as well. When others declined to do so and the truth came out, Harrick was fired. He was out of basketball for a year and searching hard to get back into coaching. URI gave him that opportunity.

Harrick spent two tumultuous years in Kingston. No one questioned his coaching ability. Using the players Skinner left behind, the Rams reached the Elite Eight and came within one minute of earning a berth in the Final Four in 1998 before losing a controversial two-point game to Stanford. It won its first and only Atlantic 10 title the following year, led by one of the players Harrick brought in, Lamar Odom.

For me, working with Harrick was very different. He was supremely confident and loved to tell stories. They were entertaining. He could be wonderfully gracious. One of the few common threads he had with Skinner was that he loved to dress well. His wife, Sally, told us stories on one road trip about how she would pick out his clothes each morning and put them out for him. He wanted to look good, and she made sure he did.

The problem with Harrick was that it became difficult to believe him when he spoke about his players and his program. There were numerous times when Harrick made statements that I knew simply were not true, including such things as the graduation rate of his players.

Harrick was so smooth he seemed to think he could get anyone to do what he wanted. Here is one such story. In his second year, URI had a late-season Saturday afternoon game at St. Bonaventure, the dreaded trip to upstate New York Atlantic 10 teams must take, one that includes a ninety-minute ride from the airport through snow-covered farmland. For such trips, I did the same thing the team did whenever possible—we stayed in Buffalo at the Millersport Marriott (the same hotel we stayed in when we covered Patriots games in Buffalo).

I was there with the team for this trip as well. I drove to Olean the morning of the game, did my work afterward, and waited to have dinner until I got back to the hotel in Buffalo. On my walk to the bar/restaurant, I passed a game room. There, playing a pinball machine—not a computer, but an old-fashioned pinball machine—was Lamar Odom. He looked like a typical teenager having fun, not one of the most highly touted basketball prospects in the country.

When I reached the restaurant, Harrick and his entire staff, including Jerry DeGregorio, Odom's mentor, and Jim Harrick Jr., were there. I sat with them. Somewhere in the conversation, I mentioned that Odom was in the game room acting like a young kid having fun. Odom was a pleasant guy to deal with, someone I enjoyed both watching play and work with before and after games. However, at that time, stories were circulating that Odom was almost certain to leave after only one year of college ball because he could go as high as number one in the draft. I said something to the effect that he could benefit as a person if he stayed in school another year, but it would be understandable if he left because so much money as involved.

Harrick shook his head.

"Don't you understand, Kenyon, that he will do whatever I want him to do?" the coach said. "I don't care what other people are saying; the only thing that matters is what I say."

Odom, of course, did leave, but only after he brought me one more memorable day. Shortly after the season finished, I received a telephone call from DeGregorio asking if I could help him. He said Tim Floyd, the coach of the Chicago Bulls who had the top pick in the draft, was coming to town in a few days. Floyd was turning it into a working vacation. He and his business manager would be with their wives and spend much of their time in Newport. But he wanted to play golf one day and talk about Odom.

As URI coach, DeGregorio had a membership at Quidnessett Country Club, one of Rhode Island's prettiest courses with several beautiful holes along the ocean. The problem was that DeGregorio had only played golf a few times in his life and he did not know Quidnessett's layout. He asked if I would play to make sure everyone knew where they were going. It was fine with me, a chance to pick up more information on Odom while playing golf.

We had a pleasant day on the course and then a nice lunch. Odom was the subject of conversation much of the day. DeGregorio, understandably, did what he could to sell Odom's good points. He cared for Odom more like a father than a coach. The two were that close.

I was honest and spoke highly of Odom much of the time. But I also pointed out how he had maturity issues and had some growing up to do. As it turned out, the Bulls chose Elton Brand with the top pick, and Odom fell to number four to the Clippers. Odom, of course, went on to a terrific NBA career, but also continued to have personal problems off the court, capped by his near-death experience in a Nevada brothel in the fall of 2015.

Harrick ended up leaving URI on the weirdest April Fool's Day I ever experienced. We were informed on that April 1 that Georgia was holding a press conference to announce it was hiring Harrick. As a bigger school in a more powerful conference, Georgia could pay more than URI could. To that point, Harrick's image had been rebuilt through his work in Rhode Island.

Mid day, URI officials called to say they were holding a press conference to announce they were giving Harrick a new contract and more money. He had agreed to stay. So, everyone headed to URI to cover the event.

We sat in the press room at URI's Mackal Forum and waited and waited. The scheduled start time came and went with no one appearing. Finally, Petro, the athletic director, and Robert Carothers, the school president, appeared. There was no Harrick. April Fool. They reported that, in effect, Georgia had outbid URI and that Harrick was leaving after all.

Since the program was in good shape, URI decided to try to continue the momentum and hired DeGregorio to succeed Harrick. DeGregorio had brought in Odom and many of the other players in the previous two years. He was a great recruiter. Unfortunately, he was not a good head coach.

His hiring turned out to be a disaster. DeGregorio was impossible not to like. A big, burly guy with an outgoing, affable personality, he had fun wherever he went. That applied most of all when he was with the players. He had been the guy most responsible for bringing them—almost all were from New York—to URI. He was their friend as much as their coach.

He was an ideal assistant coach. But he was a bad match as a head coach. Not only was he unable to establish any discipline, but he had also never been a head coach, so he struggled during games to keep up with what opponents were doing. URI went 12–48 in his two seasons. By the end, just about everyone, perhaps even including DeGregorio, knew a change was needed.

As so often happens when discipline is a problem, the response was to bring in a coach known for discipline. St. Bonaventure played in the same league as the Rams, so URI officials had gotten to know Bonnies coach Jim Baron.

He had a reputation for rebuilding downtrodden teams. He had done it at St. Francis of Pennsylvania and at St. Bonaventure. He was brought in to straighten things out at URI, and he did. He spent eleven years at Rhode Island and won at least nineteen games seven times. He went to six postseason tournaments. The problem was that they were made up of five NITs and one CBI. He never made the NCAA Tournament, which led to his departure.

For me, Baron was one of the easiest people to work with ever. He is as fine a person as you could imagine. He worked as hard as anyone I've ever been around. He was a true blue-collar guy from New York City. He was as straitlaced and straightforward as they come. His two sons, Jimmy and Billy, both of whom played for URI and are now playing in Europe, are chips off the Baron block, two of the finest young men I have ever worked with. Jimmy Baron is now among the all-time scoring leaders in URI history, a pure three-point shooter of the first order and a bright, articulate guy who certainly has a future in coaching if he so chooses.

The problem with Jim Baron, the coach, was he never won the big game. He could never get over the hump to get his team into the NCAA Tournament. From where I sat, there was one reason for that above all others: he worked too hard. Baron pushed his team hard from day one of practice. His teams were excellent in November and December. Three years in a row, his team was in position to qualify for the NCAA Tournament heading into the final month of the season.

Every time, they struggled. They had a series of close, bitter losses late in the year. Never in Baron's time at URI did one of his teams beat a school ranked in the top twenty-five. On a personal level, I grew to respect him tremendously as a person. His two top assistants, Pat Clarke and Kevin Clark, were equally good people who were of a huge help to me in doing my job.

Still, when the decision was made to part ways with Baron, it was totally understandable. It needed to be done. URI had never gone so long without getting into the NCAA Tournament. The program landed on its feet. Thorr Bjorn, the athletic director, hired Dan Hurley, of the famous New Jersey Hurley basketball family, and URI hoops have thrived ever since.

I got to work just enough with Hurley to see that he had a work ethic similar to Baron's. History has shown that he has been able to bring in better talent and build better teams. Since I have returned to my role as a fan, I no longer have to be impartial. I now can root for URI the way I did when I was in college.

Commissioner Dave Gavitt, in the foreground,
gathers the Big East basketball coaches in front
of Madison Square Garden in New York.

CHAPTER 10

THE FRIARS

As big a role as the University of Rhode Island has played in my life, Rhody basketball was not the first college team I rooted for. That would be Providence College.

For Baby Boomers growing up in Rhode Island, the Friars became our team. The Red Sox, Celtics, Patriots, and Bruins were fun, but we were only part of something bigger with the teams from Boston. We had the Rhode Island Reds, who gave us some memorable times growing up in the 1950s and '60s playing American Hockey League games in the old, smoke-filled auditorium on North Main Street in Providence.

But everything was overshadowed by Providence College's rise to prominence as we were growing up. PC played schools like Assumption, Stonehill, and Brandeis in the 1940s and '50s. But the arrival of Joe Mullaney, a young coach who had played on a national championship Holy Cross team with Bob Cousy and who had only one year of experience as a head coach, changed everything.

The University of Rhode Island had been a national power in college basketball in the World War II era with Frank Keaney's teams, the inventors of fastbreak basketball who led the nation in scoring every year but one in the 1940s. The only problem for the Rams was that they did it before anyone could hear games on the radio, let alone see them on television. It also was before college basketball grew into the spectacle that it is today.

The timing for PC and Mullaney was much better. Mullaney turned the Friars into something special as his teams put together winning records twelve years in a row. PC had the third best overall record in all of college basketball in the 1960s, behind only UCLA and Kentucky, and had nine straight seasons of twenty wins or more.

Early on in the Friars' run of success, Chris Clark, a sportscaster on one of the Providence television stations, talked his bosses into broadcasting PC games on the radio. The first game was a three-overtime thriller against powerful Villanova, and a tradition was born. All PC games were broadcast after that.

I would be one of many who went to bed as a junior high and high school student with a transistor radio on the bed stand so I could listen to Friar games. Clark told us all about the exploits of little Vinny Ernst, John Egan, and Lenny Wilkens, as well as big men Jim Hadnot and John Thompson, and then, in the mid 1960s, a great player named Jimmy Walker who would lead the nation in scoring.

It was impossible to be a sports fan and not love PC. Clark was a big factor. He was an excellent broadcaster who made everything come alive. At one point, he did so with the help of a young statistician who was still in Hope High School, a kid named Jerry Kapstein who would go on to a tremendous career in baseball as an agent, team president, and, most recently, senior adviser to the Boston Red Sox and Baltimore Orioles.

Mullaney was so good that he was lured way to the NBA, where he coached Elgin Baylor and Wilt Chamberlain with the Lakers, among many others.

I had some dealings with Mullaney in his later years when he returned to coach Brown and PC. He was, as advertised, a classy, soft-spoken, likeable man. He is the one who put Providence College on the sports map. As sports fans know, it usually is difficult to follow a legend—which is what Mullaney became in Rhode Island. As hard as it was to believe, Mullaney's successor not only was up to the challenge; he was even better. His successor was one of his assistants, Dave Gavitt.

Gavitt not only built on the success, he improved on it.

I occasionally am asked about who I felt was the most impressive person I ever worked with. As I have said earlier, Bill Belichick is the best coach. But for the overall package, for being a fabulous coach, a tremendous program builder and an absolute visionary, Dave Gavitt was the man. He had the entire package at the top level. And that extended to his personality and his way of dealing with everyone, as well.

Gavitt is in the basketball Hall of Fame, with good reason. The court Providence College now plays on in the Dunkin' Donuts Center is the Dave Gavitt Court. There has been no one in my lifetime who contributed more to his school and the state of Rhode Island than Gavitt. Compiling his lists of achievements is difficult because he did so much in so many different areas.

He would have had a great career based solely on what he did as a coach. After taking over for Mullaney, he guided PC to eight straight postseason appearances, five in the NCAA Tournament and three in the NIT. His 1973 team, led by native sons Ernie DiGregorio and Marvin Barnes, along with adopted Rhode Islander Kevin Stacom, almost certainly would win a vote among sports fans of my generation as the greatest team ever in Rhode Island. Led by DiGregorio's incomparable ball-handling and passing and Barnes's dominant inside play, the Friars had the state buzzing as they ran their way into the Final Four, the first team from New England to reach the Final Four since Holy Cross in 1947.

PC took a double-digit lead over Memphis State in the national semifinals before Barnes injured his knee and was sidelined. Memphis State came back to win, 98–85.

For Gavitt, that was only the start. In addition to coaching the basketball team, the Dartmouth grad also served as PC's athletic director from 1971 to 1982. In that role, he was able to see the big picture. He saw dramatic changes coming in college basketball before anyone else and put his vision into action.

Gavitt, helped by several others, most notably his close friend Dee Rowe, then at the University of Connecticut, went around gathering support for a new league, something that would be called The Big East. His vision was to take advantage of as many of the major media markets on the East Coast as possible and work with a new television network that was being launched at almost the same time, something called ESPN, the Entertainment and Sports Programming Network.

Since Gavitt was the prime mover, he was named the commissioner, and the headquarters was established in Providence. It is not likely that even Gavitt could have foreseen the success of the conference, which helped build Georgetown's John Thompson, Syracuse's Jim Boeheim, St. John's Lou Carnesecca, and Connecticut's Jim Calhoun into coaching legends. The conference immediately became one of the best in the nation and peaked in 1985 when three of its members, Georgetown, St. John's, and eventual champion Villanova, reached the Final Four.

As he was guiding the Big East, Gavitt became a national figure. He was asked to coach the 1980 Olympic team, but lost out on the opportunity because of the boycott of the Moscow games by the United States. Gavitt stayed on with the Olympic program and served as president from 1988–1992. It was while he was president that the concept of a "Dream Team" made up of NBA stars was put forth.

From 1982 to 1984, Gavitt was chairman of the NCAA Division I Basketball Selection Committee. It was while he was in charge that the tournament expanded to sixty-four teams, a move Gavitt said was designed to give schools from the smaller conferences a better chance to make the tournament. It was under Gavitt's guidance that the NCAA began moving some tournament games away from campus venues to the larger, domed stadiums so that more could attend.

Gavitt resigned as Big East commissioner in 1990 to become CEO of the Boston Celtics. He did that for four years before becoming president of the NCAA Foundation in 1995. He also served as chairman of the board of the Basketball Hall of Fame.

He was an amazing man, compounded by the fact that he was such a delightful, unassuming person to be around.

Gavitt also had a knack for recognizing good people. When he began the Big East, he hired Mike Tranghese, who had been working with him as the sports information director at Providence College, as his top assistant. The two worked together until Gavitt left in 1990.

Tranghese took over and did a marvelous job in keeping the Big East not only heading in the same direction, but also maintaining its image as a leader in the changing landscape of college athletics. He pushed for the addition of football schools to the conference and spoke often about how it was football, not basketball, which controlled the college landscape. There is much more money in football than in basketball. His warnings about how the Big East would not be able to continue as it had been operating came to fruition in 2003 when three members quit and joined the ACC.

Even with the setback, Tranghese did a masterful job in reshaping the conference to not only keep it viable, but maintain its position as one of the power conferences. In something of a final farewell, the Big East had three of its schools, Connecticut, Pitt, and Louisville, earn number-one seeds in in the NCAA Basketball Tournament in 2008, his final year on the job. As he left, Tranghese spoke candidly about what he saw happening with college athletics.

"When they start talking about perfect fits and academics, that's when I get turned out. That's PR gobbledygook," he said of the reasons why schools were changing conference. "With every piece of expansion, they say it's about fit and academics. I want to say, 'Don't insult my intelligence.' I think the public is just fed up with it. We're supposed to be educational institutions. Right across the board, it seems people are just jumping ship for what appears to be more money," he told the *Sporting News*.

The conference continued its Rhode Island tradition, naming John Marinatto as Tranghese's successor. I could relate to Marinatto. I have known him since he was fifteen years old. His career was much like my own in that he became involved in sports while he was in high school and never left.

Marinatto worked for us at the *Journal* as our correspondent from Our Lady of Providence Seminary. He would attend games, most notably the basketball games where Joe Hassett Sr. was the coach. Hassett Sr. was part of a great group of high school basketball coaches in the 1980s in Rhode Island, a group that included Ray Pepin, the man who built my old school, Bishop Hendricken, into the dominant power in the state; Jim Ahern at Mount Pleasant; Don Pastine at Central; Dick Rouleau at Pilgrim; and Ed Heroux at La Salle. They all were basketball lifers who ran excellent programs for their players.

Marinatto would call in box scores and provide us with enough information to do a brief story on all OLP games. He went from there less than a mile up the street to Providence College, where he was a manager for Rick Pitino with the Friars and became very close with Pitino's family. There were times when I thought Marinatto was too quiet, too pious, and even too nice to become involved in an activity where being aggressive is almost a requirement. Marinatto not only survived; he became PC athletic director, a role in which he served for fourteen years, and then Big East commissioner from 2009 to 2012. He has been blamed by some for the inability of the Big East to keep its football schools from leaving and breaking into the basketball-centric alignment it has become.

The truth is, no one could have prevented the breakup. As Tranghese predicted, the desire to chase the money was the only thing that mattered for the football schools. The conference headquarters left Providence for New York in 2014, but the impact Gavitt brought for more than three decades will go down as the greatest sports story ever in Rhode Island.

CHAPTER 11

MORE COACHES

When it comes to college basketball, Philadelphia is the unquestioned king on the East Coast. Big Five basketball in Philly is as good as it gets. Otherwise, though, Rhode Island can make a claim for being number two. Yes, ahead even of New York and Boston.

Success builds interest, and Rhode Island has had more than its share. The list of coaches and players we have had the chance to watch and work with is tremendously impressive. It was an honor to have had the chance to record some of the happenings.

URI started it all with Frank Keaney making the Rams the highest-scoring team in the country through the 1940s. Ernie Calverley, who grew up in Pawtucket and was among the game's first stars, stayed on as coach and was URI's associate athletic director when I was in school. Providence College took over as the dominant team with the arrival of Joe Mullaney and Dave Gavitt.

In the last half century, Brown and Bryant have had their time in the spotlight, and so have the Community College of Rhode Island and Rhode Island College. It brings a smile whenever I consider the people I have had a chance to work with: Rick Pitino, Rick Barnes, Pete Gillen, Tim Welsh, Eddie Cooley, Tom Carmody, Al Skinner, Jim Baron, Dan Hurley, Gerry Alaimo, Mike Cingiser, Tim O'Shea, Vin Cullen, and Bob Walsh, to name a few of the best.

Count me in the camp that believes college basketball is the coach's game, unlike the NBA, where the players dictate virtually everything. It was fascinating to see how different coaches operated and, yes, entertained, too.

A young, enthusiastic Pitino brought his Brother Rick Travelling Salvation Show to PC as documented by the great *Journal* basketball writer and columnist Bill Reynolds in his book *Born to Coach*, co-written with Pitino. His 1987 Final Four team, led by Billy Donovan, was ahead of its time in making use of a new rule that counted baskets beyond nineteen feet, nine inches as being worth three points.

Barnes had a great eye for talent, one that has continued through his career. Gillen made everyone laugh with his self-deprecating sense of humor, even after a victory. As I wrote about earlier in this section, I have tremendous admiration for Skinner and Baron for their personal character and the way they run their programs. Alaimo and Cingiser were ever true to Brown for their entire careers, their fun-loving personalities giving the Ivy League school something different than the typical dignified Ivy stereotype.

Rhode Island College, as a Division III team, often gets lost in the shadow of the Division I schools, but it has produced a run of strong teams in numerous sports under athletic director Don Tencher, none more impressive than the men's basketball program under Bob Walsh. Walsh is as well organized as any coach, and as personable as well. He has moved on to Maine to get his chance at the Division I level and has plenty of friends back in Rhode Island rooting for his team to do well.

One person who never moved up but earned a national reputation anyway was Vin Cullen. All he did was build an entire athletic program while teaching and building a hugely successful hoop program at the Community College of Rhode Island. Cullen won more than six hundred games as a coach and was New England Junior College Coach of the Year thirteen times. He contributed even more by being willing to help off the court.

Among his other roles, he was also a founding member of the National Alliance of Two Year College Athletic Administrators and served as its president in 1995. He served on that group's executive committee and as its liaison to the American Association of Community Colleges. No one has done more in our area for community colleges than Vin Cullen.

I mentioned Tim O'Shea earlier as one of Skinner's assistants at URI who helped me so much as I was beginning my work with college basketball. O'Shea went with Skinner to Boston College, left briefly to get his first head coaching job at Ohio University, but returned to his native New England to guide Bryant in its jump from Division II to Division I. It has turned out to be a perfect match.

O'Shea had the patience needed to build his program. He makes no secret of his love for Rhode Island, not just the basketball team, but life in the region. I had trouble reaching him one day, which was unusual because he was always so cooperative. It turned out he was attending the funeral of US Senator Claiborne Pell, simply to pay his respects and see the numerous national and worldwide dignitaries who came to Newport for the funeral.

O'Shea is now part of another outstanding group of college basketball coaches in the state, along with Brown's Mike Martin, URI's Hurley, and PC's Cooley. All four are former players themselves who are young enough to relate to their players but also old enough to appreciate the game and the fine history in the state. I had a chance to work briefly with Hurley and Martin before retiring and loved the way they went about their work. My history with Cooley goes back much longer and includes one of my favorite stories of how a quiet work day can get turned into a memorable one.

Cooley did that in 1988. It was late in the high school basketball season in what would turn out to be the last of the eleven years I spent covering high school sports. I was in the office one afternoon when the building guard called the sports department and said there was someone with him asking to come in to speak to me, a young man named Ed Cooley.

Cooley was then a senior at Central High. He had been an All-Stater the previous year and attended the dinner the *Journal* hosted for all the All-Staters. Because his team was the best in the state, I had covered a number of Central games and gotten to know Cooley a bit.

So, this one afternoon, Cooley came striding into the *Journal* office with a purpose. Wearing a University of Maryland jacket ("That's where I want to go," he explained), he said he was there to help. He knew I had to pick the All-State team again, and he was offering his assistance. He spoke about how knew all the best players in the state. With Bill Reynolds, our columnist and leading basketball expert in the state, joining us, Cooley proceeded to talk about players from across the state.

He was great. He did not talk about himself or the other players on his team. He really did know what he was talking about. He was mature way beyond his years.

To this day, I believe Cooley is the only high school student ever to help the *Journal* pick an All-State team. His action that day in the office turned out to be typical. Cooley went on to play for Ray Pepin, the former Hendricken coach who had gone on to Stonehill College. Cooley injured a knee and was not the same player he had been, but Pepin spoke glowingly about what a great person Cooley was for the team and the school, to the point of calling him the "Mayor of Stonehill."

After spending a couple years teaching history in high school, Cooley moved into college coaching. When he joined Al Skinner's staff for Skinner's final year at URI, I got to know him even better. He was still the same.

"I'm going to be a head coach by the time I'm thirty-five," he told me one day.

Sure enough, he was thirty-five when he was named head coach at Fairfield. Dave Gavitt would be proud of what Cooley is doing at PC these days.

CHAPTER 12

THE RIGA

While I was fortunate enough to be able to cover so many different sports for the *Journal*, there was one area that was consistent from the beginning to the end: golf.

For me, it was the best of the best. It was the sport I most enjoyed covering. The values of the game, and the people in it, helped shape my life and my own philosophy on how to live and act.

In golf, you get what you earn. There are no officials to blame, no teammates to depend on (at least, not in most events). The rules are well defined—some feel too well defined—and to be observed by everyone, even if they are sometimes complicated and difficult to understand. That is not a problem, since golf is the only sport where the participants govern themselves, up to and including calling penalties on themselves. I am among those who feel that one of the best ways to learn about a person's character is to put him or her on a golf course and see how that person acts.

I was exposed to the game as a teenager. My dad, George, and his brother, Harold, liked to play. We went to Goddard Park, the state-operated course where it cost seventy-five cents for nine holes, or to Coventry Pines. It was an enjoyable way to spend time, even if none of us played very well.

I covered my first tournaments while I was still with the *Pawtucket Times*. In one of the first events, a fourteen-year-old from Barrington named Brad Faxon won the Rhode Island Golf Association (RIGA) Junior Championship and made it look easy in the process. He looked special to me and, as everyone has learned in the last forty years, he truly is special.

It was through golf that I met Ed Duckworth, then the assistant sports editor at the *Journal* and the paper's golf writer. It led to him recommending me for a job in Providence, which would include replacing him as the *Journal's* beat writer covering RIGA events.

In the 1970s, golf was still very much a country-club game, one not always open to public course players and even more restricted for women. Rhode Island was even more closed than other states because it was so small and self-contained. The rivalries were not only among the players, but at times even more among the private clubs.

Newport, the oldest and one of the most prestigious courses in the country, the home of the first US Open and US Amateur, was the playground for only the very rich. Agawam Hunt and Sakonnet were the places where the wealthy old Yankee families belonged. Point Judith was the club for Catholics. Ledgemont and Crestwood were almost exclusively Jewish. Alpine was built to give Italians a club of their own.

Right about the time I began at the *Journal*, the paper ran a front-page story about a feud between Agawam and Point Judith, which started because an Agawam member felt he was mistreated when he played as a Point Judith member-guest because he was not Catholic. Agawam reportedly then decided to ban Point Judith members from its member-guest list.

Just as I was learning about how restrictive and snobbish some country clubs were, the game began to change for the better. Joe Sprague was taking over as the director of the RIGA from the retiring Ed Perry.

Sprague became one of my mentors, one of the people I most looked up to. He was a schoolteacher who also coached golf and hockey. He lived adjacent to Wannamoisett Country Club and spent his formative years caddying at the course. He later became a member and one of the state's leading players.

More importantly, when he became the RIGA director, he made it his mission to open the game for everyone. Using the ideals he learned as a public school educator, he campaigned in his own quiet style to bring the game to the people. A conservative, strait-laced gentleman of the first order, Sprague treated everyone as equal. He was the straightest of straight arrows. His organizational skills were superb. He turned the RIGA from a closed organization into one open for everyman.

Rhode Island had been extremely successful in golf ever since Newport CC became one of the founding members of the United States Golf Association. Players like West Warwick's Ronnie Quinn, the son of a former governor of Rhode Island, Bobby Allen, and Bob Kosten piled up numerous honors in the 1950s and 1960s, but their era was coming to an end.

Under Sprague, new stars blossomed, players who were about to create what will go down as the golden era for golf in Rhode Island. Faxon; Billy Andrade; the entire Quigley family, Paul, Dana and Brett; Eddie Kirby, Patrick Horgan and Patrick Sheehan all excelled first in RIGA events and later on the national level. The number of member courses in the association nearly doubled. New events were added, and times became better than ever. It felt like an honor just to be able to watch and report on it all.

As the association grew and prospered, it became possible to add a second full-time member of the staff. In too many ways, nepotism is a way of life in Rhode Island. Those who did not know better might have thought it was simply more of the same when Sprague hired his son, Joe Jr., to be his assistant.

Nothing could be further from the truth. The reality was that the younger Sprague was the perfect guy for the job. He was his father's son, organized, gentlemanly, and extremely competent. He had learned the game not only from his father, but also from time spent caddying on the PGA Tour after his graduation from Providence College.

Working the RIGA events was different from covering college or pro events. The participants were schoolteachers, lawyers, insurance men, dentists, electric company employees, and people from every walk of life, not to mention the high school and college students on the rise. They were competing for the joy of competing. Any recognition they might receive from the newspaper was simply a bonus.

I can't count the number of friends I made at the RIGA tournaments over the past four decades. It was the most pleasurable work possible. It did not feel like work, because the atmosphere was so pleasant. It was a joy to report not only on excellent play on the course but on classy examples of fair play demonstrated by the competitors. Guys like Paul Quigley, Nick Cioe, Tom Goryl, George Pirie, Mike Soucy, Charlie Blanchard, Dean Gregson, and a hundred others proved to be not only good players, but even better men and great sportsmen.

It was not a surprise that when the elder Sprague left after thirteen years on the job, his son took over as his successor. It might have created the smoothest transition any three thousand-member organization has ever seen.

Joe Jr., or Jay, as some call him, simply kept everything headed in the same direction his father had set. The gag among members was that the biggest change the younger Sprague made from his father's system was to let players take off their pants. Joe Sprague Sr. was such a traditionalist that he refused to allow players to wear shorts while taking part in competition, even after the USGA made such a change. The younger Sprague waited a year after taking over for his father before announcing that RIGA players could be like everyone else and wear Bermuda shorts while competing.

Fifteen years after starting with the RIGA and eight years after taking over for his father, Joe Jr. left to become the executive director for the Massachusetts Golf Association.

"Joe and his father have done so much for the RIGA. They've been one of the best tandems, I think, any sport has been lucky enough to have in Rhode Island," Don Lamb, then the RIGA president, said on Sprague's departure.

Sprague spent seven years with the MGA before moving on to the big leagues. He is now the USGA's director of regional affairs for the northeast region.

In addition to their work with golf, both Spragues also were actively involved in hockey in Rhode Island. Through his work as a goal judge for college games, Joe Sprague Jr. met Bob Ward, a schoolteacher who also worked college and Providence Bruins hockey games. They became friendly in part because Ward is also a golf guy as well as a hockey guy.

When he needed a tournament director to take over his job as second in charge, Sprague recommended Ward. Ward got the job. Ward later took over as director when Sprague left for Massachusetts.

The RIGA under Ward (with still another hockey guy, Jim McKenna, as tournament director) is very different in some ways, yet much the same in other ways. Ward is a very different personality than the Spragues. He is outgoing, talkative, and opinionated. He says more in one day than the Spragues did in a week. Under his leadership, the RIGA is louder than ever. The staid old reputation of the game is long gone.

In the most important aspects, Ward could be a member of the Sprague family. It was under his leadership that the RIGA finally was able to achieve a merger with the RIWGA, the state's women's organization. Katie DeCosta, who had been working at Wanumetonomy, a course in Middletown, Rhode Island, was hired in 2014 to be the director of women's golf and membership services, and women's participation immediately grew by leaps and bounds.

Ward, in his usual talkative style, tells anyone who asks about how having women under the RIGA umbrella has brought changes. The women, he explains, prefer different types of events than the men, more team competition than individual events. To his credit, he has not told the women they have to change. Instead, the organization has changed and embraced the preferences the women brought, and the schedule has been adjusted accordingly.

A second women's organization, the Ocean State Women's Golf Association, remains on its own. Ward wants that group as part of his organization, too. But that group has what he feels are more restrictive policies regarding participation, and his feeling is that the RIGA cannot go along with such arrangements. So, there has been no merger with that group.

Ward not only has continued the growth of the last thirty years; he has expanded it, most recently adding two clubs from Connecticut to the RIGA list: Connecticut National and Quinnatisset, both of which are within three miles of the Rhode Island state line. When some complained about players from Connecticut winning events, Ward's response was firm.

"They're members like anybody else. The more, the merrier," he said. "We welcome everyone who meets our membership requirements. The only thing I tell the guys who complain is, `If you don't like it, play better. Beat them. Compete.'"

It is all so very different from when I began. I cannot hide how I feel about what has happened. After I retired from the *Journal*, I joined the RIGA as a part-time reporter for the organization. I still write golf stories. Now, they appear on the Internet instead of the newspaper.

Billy Andrade and Brad Faxon celebrate making
another birdie in the CVS Charity Classic.

CHAPTER 13

ANDRADE AND FAXON

Timing, as any athlete knows, is everything. We've all had our lives impacted by being in the right place at the right time, or vice versa.

For me, it has been one long series of good breaks, of having the right timing, although not necessarily because of anything I did. In many ways, I have not controlled my life. Instead, because of my job, I have had to react to what others have done. Others have dictated what I have had to do. Two men, more than any others, have affected me and made my life better because of what they have done.

Brad Faxon and Billy Andrade. Or Billy Andrade and Brad Faxon.

I wrote about them more than anyone else in my career, and it's not even close. I've watched them win state championships and college awards and national championships. In large part because of them, I have covered The Masters twice and thirteen US Opens. I've met and interviewed Sandy Koufax, Bill Murray, and Glenn

Fry, not to mention having direct dealings with Arnold Palmer, Jack Nicklaus, Gary Player, and many of the other great's of the second half of the twentieth century.

It was my good fortune to arrive as the *Providence Journal's* golf writer at the same time Bristol Billy and Barrington Brad were hitting the scene, on their way to two of the greatest professional careers for any athlete in any sport in Rhode Island history. Someone had to follow and record their achievements. Of all the work I had to do in the fifty years I worked for newspapers in Rhode Island, chronicling the Brad and Billy stories was the absolute best.

I did all I could to be impartial when I was covering an event. With Billy and Brad, that became close to impossible as they moved along in their careers, both on and off the course. They are special people. As much success as they have had on the course, it does not even come close to equaling what they have given to our state off the course.

Both had excellent parental support that helped them get started, although in very different ways. Brad's parents, Brad Sr. and Linda, were constants at all his big events. The unusual part was that they were not together. They had divorced. So one would take one side of the fairway and the other would go to the opposite side. Both were totally encouraging. Brad's dad, an excellent player himself who won several statewide events, loved to talk about his son's potential. He turned out to be entirely correct that big things were in store because of Brad's uncanny touch around the greens.

Billy hails from a close family. His dad, John, who was in the insurance business, took a more low-key approach as he and his wife Helen followed Billy's exploits. At the start, even Billy's grandparents would follow him around the course. By the time

I retired, I was writing about Billy's and his wife Jody's son, Cameron, who several years ago reached the quarterfinals of the State Amateur.

Billy and Brad displayed their athletic ability in other sports. Brad was also a state champion table tennis player, a talent he liked to display to his buddies on the PGA Tour. Billy pitched his Bristol Little League team to the state championship and also was an All-State Prep basketball player at Providence Country Day School.

While they are paired in so many ways, they actually showed how junior golf was changing in their era. Brad is two years older. Junior golf was just beginning on a national scale in his teen years. Brad played few national events, instead focusing on playing both in Rhode Island and on Cape Cod, where his family had a home. His lack of national exposure showed when it came time for college. Brad dominated area events, including winning the RIGA Junior crown three years in a row before losing to his future college teammate, Eddie Kirby, in his last year of eligibility. That match, by the way, was as good as it gets as both played par golf at Metacomet before Kirby birdied the final hole to win.

Even with all he did, Faxon was lightly recruited and settled on Furman, which was not a school where a future national college player of the year would be expected to attend.

Billy, on the other hand, took advantage of the then-exploding national programs. He won what was then one of the biggest junior tournaments in the country, the Insurance Youth Classic, among others. He made such an impression at the tournament dinner that he was asked to be one of the speakers at the tournament dinner the following year, which would be his last year of eligibility to compete in the event. He did that. And, oh yes, he then went out and won the tournament again.

That made him one of the most highly recruited players in the country. He decided on Wake Forest, where he was the recipient of the Arnold Palmer Scholarship. He went on to have an excellent career for the Demon Deacons, with work that included leading the team to the national championship in his senior year.

Both were among the rare players who did not have to work their way up to the PGA Tour. They went straight there. Faxon spent time among the top ten in the world rankings. Andrade became one of the few players to win two tournaments in a row on tour.

Early in their careers, I had the opportunity to get to know them on a personal level, not only by covering their events, but also by spending time with them on the course. Back then, the *Journal* had a Sunday magazine, the *Rhode Islander*, which did in-depth features on newsmakers in the state. I was asked to do one on the two hotshot youngsters who had begun making a name for themselves on the national golf circuit.

I did some preliminary work conducting phone interviews with those who knew them, including teachers and coaches, As I was nearing the time to write the story, I asked if it was possible to meet with both men and allow some back and forth banter among the three of us. They said they were going to be home the following week and suggested meeting at Rhode Island Country Club, their home course, and we could talk as they played. They told me to bring my clubs so I could play, too.

We met as planned and were joined by one of their buddies, Willie Wood, who had been the college player of the year at Oklahoma State. It turned into a fascinating way to learn about how they had progressed to a different level than even the best amateurs.

On one hole, Billy and Brad drove within a couple yards of each other. They had almost the same distance to the hole, about 175 yards, if memory is correct. Faxon hit first and hit what most would consider a good shot, right at the stick, but about twenty-five feet short.

"It's an easy five?" Andrade asked as he got ready to hit his shot.

"No. That's what I hit. It should be a smooth five," Faxon responded.

Andrade then stepped up and drilled his shot pin high. On the way to the green, I asked what had just happened. They explained that they can hit all their irons different distances. Each club has a ten to fifteen-yard range. To get to their level, they related, a player had to be able to control distances to the yard. They could hit a six iron, say, 168 yards. Or 172 yards. Or 179 yards, if they wanted.

A few holes later, on the sixteenth, one of the beautiful holes along Narragansett Bay, I hit my approach left of the green. I was pin high, only about forty or forty-five feet from the hole, but with a bunker covering most of the distance between the hole and me. It is a narrow green, so going over would only create more problems. It was a tough shot for a good player. As it turned out, it was an impossible one for me.

I flubbed one into the bunker right in front of me. Faxon watched, and then he came over and gave me a lesson on the proper way to hit a little shot like that. Remember, this was thirty years ago, before flop shots with sixty-degree wedges. Faxon told me to change the position of my feet and change the swing path to encourage getting the ball in the air quickly and softly.

I flubbed another one. Andrade came over and made a couple suggestions. Then I skulled one over the green. They both showed me how they do and hit pretty shots within a few feet of the hole. *It's not that hard,* they insisted. They got me to try another. It was another bad shot. Faxon kept at it and was in the process of making one more try to help me, and Wood was amused watching it all and laughing. Andrade finally ended it.

"Never mind, it's hopeless," he said. "He can't do it."

The story tells much about the two. They are pleasant, affable guys to spend time with on a golf course, people willing to go out of their way to try and help someone. It also showed a difference in their personalities. Faxon is the gentlemanly, composed type who would never end the lesson the way Andrade did. He is too diplomatic. Andrade, on the other hand, is the more gregarious, outgoing, fun-loving guy who will say what he feels. He is more direct.

The two continue their careers. Faxon has shifted much of his focus to television. He still plays, but he spends much of his time as a member of the Fox Network crew, which is the new host for USGA events. Andrade is among the leading players on the Champions Tour and won the season-ending championship in 2015.

Nearly forty years later, nothing has changed. The two remain the same now as they were then, two of the most pleasant people anyone would want to spend time with, on or off a golf course.

Many players who hail from the north and reach the PGA Tour relocate to a warm-weather climate, places like Florida and Arizona, so they can work on their games all year. Faxon did that initially, moving to central Florida. He began listing his home as Florida at some tournaments and as Rhode Island in others. Officials make an issue of such matters, listing every player's hometown in programs and in announcing their names at the start and end of each round. Faxon learned that people pay attention.

"It never failed that when I was listed as from Barrington, Rhode Island, someone during the course of the tournament, no matter where the tournament was, could come up to me and want to talk about Rhode Island. There was a sense of pride. When it's Florida, no one pays attention, because so many others are from Florida," he said. It became a moot point for much of his career. He moved back to Barrington when his three daughters became school-aged.

Andrade learned of the same process and copied Faxon. His wife, Jody, is from Atlanta. When they married, they settled in Atlanta. But he also maintained a home in Rhode Island. So, to this day, when he plays on the Champions Tour, where he has had considerable success, he is sometimes from Atlanta, sometimes from Bristol, Rhode Island.

As everyone in Rhode Island knows, Andrade and Faxon have done far more for the state than play well on a golf course. We will talk about that a bit later.

CHAPTER 14

THE BIG THREE

Only once in my working career was I involved in a scene that left not only the competitor, but also everyone around him crying. It came in June 1994 at Oakmont Country Club, the scene of the US Open.

Ernie Els ended up winning the title in a playoff over Colin Montgomery and Loren Roberts. But the most memorable part of the week took place on Friday, the day the cut was made. All the attention was on Arnold Palmer.

Palmer was then sixty-four years old. He had not played in the Open in eleven years, but the USGA extended him a special exemption to compete one last time in what was a wonderful move. Oakmont is home for Palmer. He grew up in nearby Latrobe, Pennsylvania. He played in his first Open at Oakmont in 1953. He had last played in the Open in 1983 when it was at Oakmont. Having him return for a curtain call before his home fans was a public relations bonanza.

It turned out even better than anyone could have expected. In another display of good sense, the USGA had Palmer play early on Thursday and then late on Friday. By the time he trudged up the eighteenth fairway, no one was concerned about the leaderboard. The focus was entirely on one of the most beloved sportsmen this country has ever seen. The entire eighteenth fairway was lined with members of Arnie's Army. They cheered the entire march to the green, with Palmer becoming more emotional with each step.

By the time he reached the green, he was weeping. He putted out for an 81 and 158 total, which made no difference at all. He was given the special send-off he deserved.

When he entered the large media room, which was jammed with about three hundred reporters, he had a large white towel wrapped over his shoulder to wipe away the tears. He tried to speak but broke down in tears. He tried to speak again but broke down again. A veteran radio reporter who had known him for years got up, and rather than asking a question, offered what amounted to a huge thank you to Palmer for everything he had done for the game.

Palmer tried to speak again, got only a few words out, and broke down again. He buried his face in his towel and then made one more attempt to speak. It was no use. By this time, everyone in the room was emotional. Finally, Palmer got up and began walking toward the door, weeping openly. As he did, the entire room rose and gave him a rousing ovation. It was the most emotional scene I ever saw at a sporting event.

I was sitting with Bruce Vittner, the editor of the *Ocean State Golf Magazine*. Bruce had been working with his fellow Johnston High school teacher, Dave Adamonis Sr., in putting out the magazine, one of a host of terrific projects brought to the game by Adamonis. Adamonis was leaving to launch a golf program at Johnson & Wales University in Miami, so Vittner was taking over the magazine. This was his first major tournament, his first major press conference.

"Is this what's it's always like?" Vittner said, only half in jest.

To this day, Bruce and I speak about that moment and how special it was. We get to do it often since I now work for Bruce with the magazine, now called *Southern New England Golfer*.

Palmer remains one of the truly special people I have ever had the opportunity to meet. He has a charisma that is unmistakable, that seeps from every pore. When you meet him, the surprise is that he is not big. He was listed at five foot ten through his career, although he seemed smaller than that. But he has huge, strong hands. Shaking his hands was much like doing the same thing with a three hundred-pound football lineman. He looks everyone in the eye and has a magnetism that is undeniable.

We were fortunate to get to spend considerable time with him late in his career. He played regularly in the Bank of America Champions Tour event at Nashawtuc Country Club in Concord, Massachusetts. He designed the TPC Boston course in Norton, Massachusetts, which is used for the Deutsche Bank Tournament in the PGA Tour playoffs. And, of course, he played in the CVS Charity Classic at Rhode Island Country with one of his proteges, Billy Andrade. Palmer played at the CVS in both 2002 and 2004.

One of the scenes I will remember most came in 2004. Play for the first day had been completed, and most people were getting ready for the gala held that evening. Someone came looking for Palmer. He had not yet come in. At age seventy-four, he was out on the practice range because he was unhappy with the way he had played.

He is an amazing man.

The good news for golf fans is that he did not have to build the game by himself. He was part of a "big three" that created a golden age for golf. Jack Nicklaus and Gary Player are very special, too. Those of us in Rhode Island got to see a different side of the Nicklaus family through the Northeast Amateur, the event held at Wannmoisett in late June every year.

Two of the Nicklaus sons, Jack II and Gary, each competed in the Northeast five times. Bill Lunnie, who at that time was chairman of the Northeast, loves to tell stories about how their parents were like so many other parents he dealt with through the years. That is, they were heavily involved in supporting their sons' careers, keeping in constant contact and doing it all in the right way. Lunnie speaks glowingly about Barbara Nicklaus, in particular, and the way she deals with everyone. Both sons stayed involved in the game, Gary earning his PGA Tour card at one point and Jack II becoming involved in his father's golf course architecture business.

Jack Nicklaus carries himself as modestly as any superstar. He set so many records, yet never gave in to the bigheadedness that affects so many. Actually, it was exactly the opposite. One of the reasons he agreed to compete in the CVS was that organizers told him he could partner with Gary. Everyone in the family exudes class.

Player was special in his own right, too, both on and off the course. I had one meeting with him that told me what kind of person he was. It was in 2001, when Player was headed to RICC to partner with Faxon in the CVS event. Player at the time was sixty-six years old but still working out and looking tremendously fit. He was competing in the Bank of America Champions Tour event at Nashawtuc shortly before the CVS. I sought him out to do a pre-tournament feature on him. I caught up with him shortly after he had finished play in the first round. I introduced myself and told him that I hoped to speak with him.

"I'd like to help, but I have to be …" He obviously had plans. But, even as he started to say he could not do it, he caught himself and said, "If it helps Brad and Billy, let's do it right now."

We found a place to sit, and he patiently and pleasantly answered questions about a career that made him the world's most traveled athlete, about his part in the game's "big three," and about agreeing to go to Rhode Island for a charity tournament.

He was outstanding. It said so much about him as a person. Oh, by the way, when he did come to the CVS, he sank a birdie putt on the last hole to tie him and Faxon for the title with the team of Nick Price and Mark Calcavecchia. Price won it for his team with a birdie on the first playoff hole, but Player proved he was a true champion, too, in more ways than one.

CHAPTER 15

TIGER WOODS

It was in April of 1995 when Tiger Woods took steps to explain his ethnicity to everyone and attempt to dismiss it as an issue.

Woods played in The Masters that April, his first professional major. He was still an amateur, a freshman at Stanford University who already had won one US Amateur title. Before The Masters began, Woods did all he could to explain his background to everyone, and thus hopefully dismiss it as an issue. He wanted to focus only on golf. He released a statement to the media explaining that his father, Earl, was African-American, while his mother, Kutilda, was from Thailand and part Thai and part Chinese. There also were Native American Indian and Dutch relatives in his ancestry. Woods later labeled himself "Cablinasian," a word he made up as a combination of the words Caucasian, black, Indian, and Asian.

Four months after his appearance at Augusta, where he tied for forty-first and won low amateur honors (he finished eight strokes behind Faxon that week), Woods came to Rhode Island to defend his US Am crown. The event, the one hundredth, was held at the same course where the first Amateur and Open were held, Newport Country Club.

Most will remember the week as the second of the three US Amateurs Woods would win. My memories are a bit different. As someone who enjoys studying and learning about people every bit as much as watching them perform, that week will go down as one of the most fascinating of my life. It was all because of Woods. He was the most impressive nineteen-year-old I have ever met in my life.

As the defending champion and the hot new name in the game, Woods was the player in demand. It turned out that he met with us eight days in a row in the tent set up for interviews between the first tee and ninth green. The interviews were excellent because there were never more than a dozen reporters meeting with him, some days as few as seven.

It began with one of the more memorable sessions I ever attended. One of the reporters that day was John Gearan, the sports columnist for *Worcester Telegram*. Gearan was a veteran, someone who had covered most of the top sports stories in New England for more than twenty years. He was a terrific writer with a feisty, at times combative, personality.

Gearan was there to write about this phenom, Tiger Woods. Very early in the interview, after Woods had answered a few basic questions about defending his title, Gearan asked Woods if he would explain his ethnicity. The exchange that followed went something like this:

"I dealt with that at Augusta. I handed out a sheet to explain it," Woods responded.

"Well, I wasn't at Augusta. Could you talk about it now?" Gearan asked.

"No. I'm done with that. I'm here to play golf," Woods shot back.

"Not everybody goes to Augusta. I'm here now asking you the question," Gearan said.

The exchange went on for several minutes, with Gearan pressing the issue firmly and Woods, equally firmly, refusing the discuss it. My personal reaction was that both handled themselves well. There was no right or wrong. Gearan was just doing his job. Woods was doing what he felt was best for him.

I was not particularly happy at the time, because Woods became agitated. When the questions returned to golf, he seemed less than pleased to be there, and he answered everything curtly. I remember chatting with other reporters when it was over and saying something about how this was going to be a long week if we had to deal with this every day.

Instead, it turned into a great week as everyone focused only on golf once play began. Woods was guarded for the next day or two. But as the week went on—and he kept winning—the interviews became outstanding. Remember, this was a nineteen-year-old kid who had just finished his freshman year in college. He was as articulate and as personable as any professional athlete could be. It was clear he had a lot going for him off the course, as well as on. His charisma was unmistakeable.

An added bonus that week was that Woods's father, Earl, was a constant presence, and he was happy to talk. These were the days, remember, when the elder Woods already was predicting his son would break Jack Nicklaus's record for most majors won and would take over as not only the most famous name in golf, but in the world.

"Tiger will do more than any other man in history to change the course of humanity," was Earl Woods's famous quote in an interview with *Sports Illustrated*. At one point, the elder Woods even said his son could become president of the United States if he was so inclined. Such talk would be foolish for anyone else. But after spending a full week seeing Tiger up close and personal, it did not sound foolish at all. He was that impressive.

But Woods's mannerisms and actions off the course became complicated. Less than two years after winning at Newport, he made a less-than-favorable impression with some Rhode Islanders when he refused to sign a golf ball for a collection being made for charity as part of the CVS Charity Classic. Arnold Palmer helped, and Jack Nicklaus, and every Masters champion. But not Tiger Woods.

It has been entertaining through the years to be at a Woods press conference, whether it was at a US Open or the Deustche Bank Classic held in Norton, Massachusetts, which Woods won with the lowest Sunday score of his career. He remains as articulate and quick on his feet in a press conference as any athlete I have ever encountered. There is no doubt he is unique.

As others have documented, he has done much for the game. His presence on the PGA Tour allowed purses to multiply, benefitting everyone involved. His foundation has raised so much money that it is credited with helping more than 10 million people.

At the same time, though, Woods has proved all too human with his behavior off the course. His personal foibles have badly stained his image to the point where it is difficult to imagine him becoming the humanitarian his father wanted him to be. It was easy to see why he will go down as one of the most memorable personalities of our era. He has done so much. But he has the ability to do so much more.

Brad Faxon and Billy Andrade announce distribution of more than million dollars to charities in Southern New England, the proceeds from the CVS Charity Classic.

CHAPTER 16
THE CVS CHARITY CLASSIC

As good as they have been on the course, the biggest mark Andrade and Faxon will leave on Rhode Island is the assistance they have brought to so many charities in southern New England. They are humanitarians above all else. In this day and age, when so many professional athletes make headlines for all the wrong reasons, Faxon and Andrade have gone above and beyond to do good work.

Golf prides itself on how much charitable work is done through tournaments at all levels. The game encourages charitable events. Players and tournaments raise tens of millions of dollars each year for charity. Few, though, have gone to the lengths Faxon and Andrade have.

They picked up the ball early in their careers. They put together an event at Firefly, a par-three course, in which they held a men-against-women team match against the great JoAnne Carner, an LPGA Hall of Famer who spent part of her life in Rhode Island (and used to own the Firefly course with her husband, Don), and Kay Cockerill, a UCLA product who won the US Women's

Amateur at Rhode Island Country Club. It went well and turned out to be just the opening act.

Faxon and Andrade organized their own charitable foundation, the Andrade Faxon Charities for Children. It was founded in 1990 with the mission statement of giving back to the people of Rhode Island and southeastern Massachusetts who have supported them over the years. The charity makes awards to organizations that benefit the needs of children.

To raise money for their foundation, they set up their own one-day tournament. Friends and members of their committee include members at Wannamoisett Country Club, one of Rhode Island's greatest courses. The club agreed to allow use of the facility one day each year.

A tournament was set up in which businesses could buy a foursome for $10,000. Many of the biggest businesses in the state agreed to participate, in part because by that point, many of the executives had gotten to meet Faxon and Andrade and see what kind of people they were. The other attraction for the businesses was that they would get to play golf with celebrities from all walks of life.

Their visibility on the PGA Tour allowed Andrade and Faxon to make friends with celebrities from many different fields, sports and entertainment, in particular. Faxon and Andrade are huge sports fans, so they happily got to meet and deal with stars from every sports team in Boston. As part of their play on tour, they also got to meet movie stars, musicians, and politicians. They decided to call on their friends to provide them a great day of golf, all expenses paid, if they agreed to come to Wannamoisett and play with business leaders.

Faxon loves the Eagles rock group. He and Glenn Frey, one of the leaders of the Eagles, became good friends, to the point where Frey once caddied for Faxon in the Masters Par-3 Tournament. Frey became a regular in the Andrade-Faxon charity event. The list of participants was awesome. Bill Murray took part several times, bringing his *Caddyshack* persona. Sandy Koufax might have been the biggest hit and most popular player of all. Joe Pesci played, as did Bobby Orr, Andre Tippitt, Roger Clemens, Charles Barkley, and numerous others. Some of the businessmen who took part tell stories about what a great time they had at the event. The event was not publicized beforehand; thus, Wannamoisett members who wanted to attend were the only observers.

The day ended with a dinner and charity auction, usually hosted by sportscasters Chris Berman or Sean McDonough, at which items were auctioned off to raise more money. The event made national headlines in a roundabout way in 1997 when one of the items auctioned was a display case that contained golf balls autographed by every living Masters Champion. Well, all except one. Tiger Woods refused to sign.

Andrade and Faxon were not shy about telling everyone that Jack Nicklaus signed and Arnold Palmer did, too. So did everyone, except Tiger. Reporters from around the country picked up the story. Two youngsters from South Kingstown, Drew and Dixon Simmons, had gotten an autographed ball from Woods two years earlier when Woods was in the process of winning the US Amateur at Newport. They contacted Andrade and Faxon and donated the ball so the display case was complete.

Glenn Frey and Joe Pesci bid on the case at the tournament auction and won when they agreed to pay $6,000. Then they promptly donated the display case to the Simmons brothers. It turned out to be one of the first examples of the way Tiger sometimes feels above the crowd. He never did sign a ball for the display.

Faxon and Andrade play down that story. Instead, they love to tell stories about how so many celebrities gave to their charity after taking part. One of the best is one Faxon tells about how shortly after the tournament at Wannamoisett, he was playing in a tour event in Chicago. When he was in the clubhouse, he saw Murray sitting and chatting with Jeff Sluman, his regular partner in the old Crosby Clambake at Pebble Beach.

Later, when Faxon returned to the locker room, there was an envelope taped to his locker. When Faxon opened it, a check fell out, with a note.

"Had a great time at your tournament," it read. It was from Murray. The check was a major donation Andrade-Faxon Children's Charities.

The charity has raised more than $7.5 million, some of which is being kept in escrow so that donations can continue for many years to come.

The charity tournament is no longer held, because Andrade and Faxon have gotten involved in an even bigger event, the CVS Charity Classic.

Among the many businessmen Faxon and Andrade met through golf was Tom Ryan, the CEO of the Rhode Island-based CVS Corporation. Ryan is a golfer and an avid sports fan, even if he sometimes roots for the wrong teams. (He grew up in New Jersey and came to Rhode Island to attend pharmacy school at URI.) Faxon and Ryan became close friends to the point where they became regular partners in the PGA event at Pebble Beach.

CVS was on its way to becoming a Fortune 400 company. It got involved in sponsoring golf events on both the PGA and LPGA Tours. The company founders, brothers Stanley and Sidney Goldstein, were golf guys, too. Faxon and Andrade had taken part in the Shark Shootout, Greg Norman's event held in Florida, and the Fred Meyer Challenge organized by Peter Jacobsen in his hometown of Portland, Oregon. They were two of the most successful small-field charity events in the country.

The idea of handpicking a small field (twenty players) appealed to the CVS people, although they decided to modify the format used at other events. They decided they would not only ask some of the current stars to take part, but also try to bring some of the great names in golf history. The thought of having Arnold Palmer or Jack Nicklaus or Gary Player walking the fairways of the course they grew up on was enticing. To their credit, they pulled it off even more successfully than they hoped.

Palmer, Nicklaus, and Player all took part, at times partnering with the co-hosts. Lee Trevino played, too, as did the classy Nick Price (who won the event three times with three different partners), Bubba Watson, Jay Haas, and Davis Love III, among many others. I was standing near the practice tee one year when Steve Pate, a first-time participant, came down to hit balls. Not long after, he went over to speak with Faxon and Andrade. Pate was looking at the ocean to his right, the beautiful clubhouse to his left, and the finishing holes along the bay.

"This place is great," he said with a bit of surprise in his voice. As with so many others before him, he came to help charity and earn a minimum of $30,000 for two days of play. He learned when he arrived how good the course was and how well the tournament was run.

The event has been ongoing since 1999 and has become the biggest annual sporting event held in Rhode Island in terms of raising money for charity. As with all new events, at its start, the tournament was looking for something to draw the attention of television viewers. The event at the beautiful bayside course was on ESPN and later on The Golf Channel.

Magic happened on the first day in the first year. Among the prizes was a car if anyone was able to make a hole-in-one on the short seventeenth, the course's signature hole only yards off the bay. In the first round, Lee Janzen aced it. Amazingly, the next player up on the tee in the same foursome, Scott McCarron, spun his shot back into the hole, too.

Two aces in one minute. It made national news and was the highlight on televised sports programs around the country. Right away, everyone knew about this new event in Rhode Island. No one has looked back since.

Faxon and Andrade, along with Peter Jacobsen's company, which organizes and runs the event, has had uncanny success in keeping the event fresh. The biggest change, made a decade after the event began, was adding LPGA stars. Morgan Pressel combined with Jay Haas to win the event in 2012.

Pressel has been a regular participant, as have Juli Inskter, Suzann Pettersen, and Lexi Thompson. The women have been a tremendous addition. Having rising stars, Champions Tour players, and LPGA stars all taking part in the same event makes it unique on the current landscape. Other events have come and gone, but the CVS tournament goes on, even as the company has had a change in leadership from Ryan to Larry Merlo.

While the event awards $1.5 million to the players for two days' work, it also brings in huge money for charity, thanks to its sponsors. The sponsors are primarily the companies CVS does business with in its stores. For their support, sponsors like Pepsi, Johnson & Johnson, and Bayer are able to play in events held at other courses before the tournament begins, play in the pro-am at RICC, and take part in the tournament gala the evening after the first round. The gala annually raises hundreds of thousands of dollars.

It is almost taken for granted these days that the event will raise over $1 million each year for area charities. The event has helped thousands in need, all because two golfers wanted to give something back to their community.

They are two very special people.

CHAPTER 17

THE MAJORS

Imagine that someone gave you a choice of two delicious things to eat. Would you prefer steak or lobster? For dessert, will it be chocolate cake or ice cream?

In golf, would you prefer to go to The Masters every year, or would you rather see the US Open at a different course every June?

As it turns out, Jim Donaldson and I have different ideas of what would be the best choice, both at dinner and in covering one of the game's great events. Jim made no secret of the fact that going to Augusta every year, seeing the same people, spending five days in golf heaven, and reporting on the premier golf event in the world was his choice.

I was an Open guy. I loved the fact that each year it was in a different part of the country, with the only constant being that every place the USGA went was superb.

The majors truly are different for the players, the measuring stick they use to separate the good from the great. It is the same for reporters. The majors are one cut above. And they create special memories. The good news for me is that I was able to get a taste of The Masters and the PGA, as well, in addition to covering thirteen US Opens.

The Providence Journal afforded us the best of both worlds. In many ways it was, and is, a small-town paper. The accomplishments of local athletes are celebrated, much more than in a big city paper where there are too many locals to deal with individually. Yet, the paper also was big enough that it paid to send reporters to the major events, from the World Series and Super Bowl to the golf majors. Unlike the big guys who often sent two, three, or even more reporters to the big events, the *Journal* more often than not settled for one at a time. That's where we had to make the choice. I was the golf writer, and Jim was one of the columnists, the one who loved golf.

It worked out great because we both got to do what we most wanted. It was even better for me because I was able to cover The Masters twice before Jim became a columnist, in 1982 when Craig Stadler won and in 1985 when Bernhard Langer took his first.

The Masters really is one of a kind. The place is nothing short of magnificent. The way everyone is treated, players, media, and fans alike, is the absolute best. I loved the time I spent there. Still, I was happier to have the opportunity to go to Pebble Beach (twice), Pinehurst, Shinnecock Hills (twice), Oak Hill, and The Country Club, among others.

The memories of the Open extend beyond the competition. The host clubs all are so different. They present very different challenges. The way the USGA sets up the course went through

118

stages. When I began covering, there were constant complaints about the rough being too deep (especially at Oakmont) to the greens being too severe (there was the crazy scene at Shinnecock where balls were rolling off greens, so the USGA watered greens to slow them down).

One reason it was an easy decision for *Journal* editors to have a reporter at the Open was because there almost always was a Rhode Islander, or two or three, taking part. It began in 1983. Brad Faxon had just finished an outstanding career at Furman, where he was the college player of the year. He was still an amateur when he qualified for the Open at Oakmont.

Faxon posted a 77 in the first round and played late on the second day, one of the last on the course. He knew that even with extremely high scores overall, he had to play better to make the cut. He did. He came to the final hole knowing he needed a par to make the cut. He was faced with a twelve-footer to save the par and, with the course nearly empty with darkness near, rolled it straight in the hole.

He ended up winning low amateur honors, with help from his father. The Open finished that year, as it always does, on Father's Day. Faxon decided he would like to spend the day with his father and asked Brad Sr. to caddie for him. Larry Nelson won the Open that day, but the bigger story I wrote about for the *Journal* was how the Faxons spent Father's Day.

Faxon also helped make for an interesting day in 1990, when the event was at Medinah in Chicago. He had an early tee time in the first round, which allowed me to do two things at once. I wanted to see the course, as usual, and I wanted to write about Faxon. With him playing so early, I could follow him through his day and then worry about writing the overall tournament story later.

There were few people around early in the morning. Early in the round, maybe the third or fourth hole, I noticed two guys following Faxon's group, guys Faxon acknowledged. It was Mark McGwire, who was, at the time, baseball's reigning home-run king. At one point later when our paths crossed, I introduced myself to McGwire and asked why he was there. He spoke about how he had become friendly with both Brad and Billy Andrade. The Athletics were in Chicago, so he wanted to come out and see Brad play in the Open. Faxon and Andrade later told stories about how McGwire could hit a golf ball longer than anyone on the PGA Tour.

The year before Medinah, when the Open was at Oak Hill in Rochester, New York, proved another great week of work. Faxon's Furman teammate, Eddie Kirby, had qualified for the Open. Cumberland Eddie, who made the tour for a year, posted back-to-back rounds of 70 to begin and was in the top fifteen at the halfwayway point. Midway through the third round, Kriby's name got on the leaderboard. I decided I had to chase him. I headed out toward the twelfth hole, where he was, and heard a huge roar as I was nearing the green. Kirby had just holed out from the fairway for eagle on the par-four and now was in a tie for sixth.

Kirby struggled with a couple bogeys coming in but still was in great position going into the final round. He drew a pairing with Greg Norman, the biggest name in the game at the time. Both struggled to 76s and finished in a tie for thirty-third with Faxon, among others. When it was over, a couple of us chased Kirby down in the locker room. He was sitting in front of his locker, clearly unhappy. When we asked about his day, he was direct and candid.

"I'm mad at myself," he began. "I let him intimidate me. All day, all I was worried about was not upsetting Greg. He never said a word to me all day. He treated me like I wasn't even there. When he finished, he'd walk off greens. I'm mad at myself for not speaking up for myself. It was the biggest day of my career, and I let him ruin it for me."

As we were speaking, Norman came walking past and saw us.

"Nice meeting you, Eddie. Good luck down the road," he said.

"Yeah, sure," was all Kirby said as he shook his head.

Seeing Payne Stewart sink a putt on the seventy-second hole to edge Phil Mickelson at Pinehurst was one of the greatest moments of all. Chasing Curtis Strange and Nick Faldo around The Country Club in Brookline, Massachusetts, in the playoff for the 1988 Open title was fun, not exactly hard work. Witnessing Tiger Woods's masterful, record-setting triumph, where he won by fifteen at Pebble Beach was the single most impressive performance these eyes have ever seen.

There are so many highlights. Fuzzy Zoeller waving his towel at Norman on the eighteenth hole at Winged Foot; almost getting in the way when Hale Irwin ran around the final green to high-five fans at Medinah; hearing the massive roar when Corey Pavin hit his famous four-wood to win at Shinnecock in 1995; seeing the joy of Rhode Island's Rodney Butcher when he made the cut at Congressional—they all are special memories of special events.

I only covered one PGA Championship, but it turned out to be one of the most historic of all. Davis Love III was being labeled the best player never to win a major. As Love was on his way to making a birdie on the final hole to finally win his major, a very visible rainbow appeared over the green, leading media to ask Love if he was thinking about his dad, also a golf pro, and if he felt he was celebrating in heaven.

If there is one golf memory that stands above all the others, for me it comes from a pseudo-major, the 1999 Ryder Cup at The Country Club. For pure drama and excitement, the historic rally by Ben Crenshaw's US team was the equal of anything I've ever seen in any sport.

A day that began with people poking fun at the shirts the United States team was wearing ended with the Americans rallying from a 10-6 deficit to a 14 ½ - 13 ½ victory, fulfilling a prediction made by Crenshaw the previous day.

In that one, the individual game turned into an unforgettable team victory. Justin Leonard's putt that won it on the seventeenth green is the big memory for many, but those of us who were there got to see a daylong string of superb shots put together by David Duval, Steve Pate, and Jim Furyk, among others. Then the champagne celebration by the players on the porch of the clubhouse turned it into one of the greatest shows ever.

CHAPTER 18

THE NORTHEAST AMATEUR

For some time now, Northeast Amateur time in late June has been one of my favorite weeks of the year. It is one idea cooked up in Rhode Island that has become more successful than even its founders could have imagined.

The list of champions in the event, held at Wannamoisett Country Club, reads like a "who's who" in the game. Ben Crenshaw, John Cook, Hal Sutton, David Duval, Luke Donald, and Dustin Johnson all won the Northeast. So did Scott Hoch, Jay Sigel, Brett Quigley, Notah Begay, Jonathan Byrd, Anthony Kim, and Peter Uihlein.

So many more played but did not win. Tiger Woods withdrew after playing only nine holes because he was ill with what turned out to be mononucleosis. Jordan Spieth finished twenty shots behind Uihlein when Uihlein set the scoring record of fifteen under in 2011. Jason Day tied for ninth in 2006. Corey Pavin, Tom Lehman, Fred Couples, and Jeff Sluman all came to Wannamoisett while they were in college, among many, many others.

It is an event that began modestly. It was the early 1960s, when Arnold Palmer was bringing the game to the masses and golf was just arriving as a popular sport. It so happened that it also was a time when the Providence Chamber of Commerce wanted to sponsor an event that would attract interest in the Greater Providence area.

Paul Mackesey was the athletic director at Brown University and also was chairman of the recreation committee for the Greater Providence Chamber of Commerce. The sports information director at Brown at the time was Pete McCarthy, a former *Providence Journal* sportswriter who just happened to live across the street from Wannamoisett. McCarthy had covered golf for the paper and loved the game.

When they were throwing around ideas about what the Chamber could do to bring people to Greater Providence, McCarthy suggested a golf tournament that would be open to all amateurs in the nation. He and Mackesey went to Ed Perry, the director of the Rhode Island Golf Association, and Perry helped arrange to get the event off the ground.

It was a hit right away, although more of a regional than national event. Dick Siderowf of Connecticut, New York's Gene Francis, and Rhode Island's Ronnie Quinn, all among the very best players in the region, were among the early champions.

Everything exploded in 1973 thanks to Ben Crenshaw. Crenshaw, fresh off winning his third straight NCAA individual title, listened to the pleas of Bob Kosten, one of Rhode Island's great players who had become the tournament chairman, to come to Wannamoisett. He accepted and won the event by seven, including a course record 65 in the final round.

Crenshaw gave the event national visibility, and it has been one of the biggest amateur events in the country ever since. Crenshaw is one of many pleasant memories for me, even though I was not there when he won the tournament. In 1986, when the event was to celebrate its twenty-fifth anniversary, I wanted to do something about the history of the tournament. Crenshaw was the obvious story. So, at the US Open held at Shinnecock Hills on Long Island, just before the Northeast, I chased Crenshaw down in the locker room, introduced myself, and asked him if he would help with his memories of Wannamoisett and the Northeast.

Crenshaw perked up immediately.

"Wannamoisett? I love that place. The Northeast? What a great event that is," he said. But then he shook his head and said he was sorry but he had an appointment and had to run. I asked if we could do it another day. The tournament began the next day, so I thought I was in trouble. He might want to focus only on getting ready for the national championship. But I was happily surprised.

Crenshaw had a late tee time, so he suggested we meet on the porch outside the clubhouse at 10:00 a.m. I happily accepted, although I must admit I had bad experiences in other sports where an athlete would put an interview off to another day and then not appear.

No such problem with Crenshaw. Actually, just the opposite happened. It led to one of the most enjoyable and helpful interviews I ever was involved in. Crenshaw showed up right on time and suggested we sit on rocking chairs on the porch and chat.

He was amazing. This was thirteen years after he had won the Northeast. He recalled specific shots he'd hit. He detailed almost every hole and spoke about course design, which was an interest that led to his forming his own golf course architecture company. He spoke about the family he stayed with, the Carrs. His recall was almost total.

It is one of many reasons I love golf so much. The people in it are so aware of all that happens around them. Golf memory is strong. A player's personality is there for all to see. At the Northeast, Wannamoisett members get to see what each person is like. The stories are legendary.

Fred Couples was the top college player in the national when he came. He did not play well when he competed in 1980, finishing twelve shots behind Hal Sutton, who won that year. As the stories go, Couples was introduced to the night life in Newport before the tournament began. He spent more time there making new friends than he spent at Wannamoisett. His host at the tournament, Jake Conley, one of the patriarchs at the club, asked Couples what he was majoring in at Houston. Couples reportedly gave Conley a funny look.

"Golf, Mr. Conley," he said. "I'm there for the golf."

Coming from someone else, that might not have gone over well. Coming from Couples, who was so pleasant, so personable, it was understandable.

While the college stars dominate the tournament, one of the aspects that make the tournament even better than others is that the best older amateurs in the country make it a regular habit to take part. Allen Doyle, who won in 1993, Buddy Marucci, Bob Lewis, Bill Hadden, and Tim Jackson were players who added class to the event for years. Todd White and Nathan Smith have taken over that role in recent years.

Still, the king in that department was Jay Sigel. An insurance man from Pennsylvania, he played in the event eighteen times in the 1980s and '90s and won three times. If you wanted to draw up the ideal golfer, with how he carries himself, how he treats those around him, and the way he plays, Sigel could be the model. He went out of his way to get to know everyone, to call everyone, right down to the bartender, by his or her first name.

A nine-time Walker Cupper before he turned pro and had a successful run on the Champions Tour (with eight victories), Sigel so impressed everyone at Wannamoisett that he was made an honorary club member.

It was also at the Northeast where I saw what goes down in my memory as the single best golf shot I have ever seen, from Notah Begay in 1995. Begay was an All-American at Stanford, although somewhat lost in the shadow of one of his teammates, Tiger Woods.

Begay came from behind with a closing 65 to win the title. It was his next-to-last shot that goes down as one of the greatest in Northeast history. Playing ahead of the leaders, he had surged to the top going four under through 17. He led by one as he played the eighteenth. His approach on the par-four went into the deep rough right of the green. He was only about forty-five feet from the hole, but with his ball nestled deep in the long grass. The pin was back center, the traditional Sunday placement. It meant Begay had to get it up and over one big mound, but not hit it so hard as to go over a second big mound on the other side of the hole.

Begay began practicing chip shots. But then he stopped, said something to his caddie, took out another wedge, and began taking full, hard swings. Remember, this was 1995, before the flop shot became fashionable. As Begay later explained, he had begun practicing flop shots but had never hit one in tournament play.

His first gave him the championship. He took a huge swing, and the ball went as high in the air as it did far. It landed gently just over the first mound and came to rest only a couple feet from the hole. He made the putt for par.

"I've been practicing that shot," Begay said later. "This was the perfect setup to use it. I told myself if I've been working on it, this was the time to prove I could do it." He won with a truly championship shot.

The men who have guided the event through the years, Kosten, Gene Voll, Bill Lunnie, Denny Glass, and now Ben Tuthill, have ensured that the event hss been at the top of the amateur ranks for more than a half century. Ron Balicki, the late longtime writer for *Golfweek* magazine, covered the event for more than two decades.

He dubbed The Northeast "The Masters of Amateur Golf." I wish I had thought of that. It is the ideal description.

CHAPTER 19

BUTTON HOLE

For the vast majority of my career, I was a reporter. It was my job to cover an event and tell people what happened. That is not to be confused, of course, with a columnist whose job it is to offer his opinion, to explain what took place, and even to advocate for an issue.

If there was one time in my career where I did some advocating, it was with Button Hole. I'm happy I did it. It turned out to be one of my proudest moments.

The Button Hole Children's Course and Teaching Center is a nine-hole par-three course built in an old gravel pit on the Providence-Johnston line. The story of how it came about is one everyone involved should be proud of.

Ed Mauro is the man who made it all happen.

Mauro is a prominent and highly successful businessman who was retirement age when he undertook the project. He did so at the urging of David Fay, the former executive director of the United States Golf Association. Mauro was an outstanding golfer in his prime, a former State Amateur champion (1965) and president of the RIGA (1997). He also served on several USGA committees, which is how he met Fay. The two became good friends, in part because of geography.

Fay liked to spend parts of the summer at the beach areas in southern Rhode Island, which is where Mauro lived. Mauro got Fay to play at his home course, Point Judith Country Club, which is in the heart of the beach area.

In the 1990s, the USGA launched a "For the Good of the Game" initiative, a program directed specifically at children, most notably those who would not otherwise be exposed to the game. Fay suggested to Mauro that perhaps Rhode Island could do something as part of the initiative.

Mauro took him up on it—and then some. Mauro, who is a bundle of energy, especially when involved in a project he cares about, went above and beyond. He put together a committee to study the matter and went to work.

One of the first moves was to see if it was possible to get land donated for such a project. Mauro's group wrote to every recreation director in every town and city in Rhode Island to explain the proposed project and ask if the community might be able to donate land. About a dozen communities responded, most saying how great the project seemed to be and how they might be able to come up with a possible site in their city or town.

Armed with good news, Mauro began seeking backers. Raising money obviously was the main priority, but Mauro was savvy enough to know that help from the media could provide a boost.

Rhode Island being the small city-state it is, Mauro felt getting positive publicity could act as a rallying point.

Among the first calls he made was one to the *Providence Journal* to seek out Jim Donaldson, one of our columnists, and me. He asked if we would like to play golf one day with him at Point Judith and, as part of the day, listen to an idea he had. Jim and I did not need to be convinced. We set a date at Point Judith, where we played with Ed and Tim Harrington, one of his right-hand men on the project. They told us a bit about their idea on the course, but then poured it on heavily over lunch.

Our reaction, to be honest, was skeptical. This was a major project, one that would cost into seven figures. Could that much money be raised in the small world of Rhode Island golf? And could a suitable site be found? Still, there was enough there to write about. I did a weekly golf round-up column in those days and related Mauro's hopes in one of my next columns.

The reaction was universally positive. A number of people volunteered to help. The more work that was done, the more realistic the project became. I never outright advocated for the project, as a columnist would do. But I came pretty close. Never in my career did I write as much about a proposed facility than I did about Button Hole. (The name came from Rhode Island's industrial past.)

The enthusiasm for the project grew even more when a decision was made on where to locate it. Several suburban communities offered peaceful plots of land that would have been ideal. Mauro thanked everyone, but selected instead an abandoned gravel pit on the Providence-Johnson line. It was sandwiched between two housing projects in one of the poorest parts of the state.

Some were not happy when they learned of the decision, insisting that it could not be done there, that it would be ruined as soon as it was built. Mauro insisted otherwise. More than twenty-five thousand disadvantaged children live within three miles of the facility.

"This is where it has to go. This is what it is all about, helping kids who otherwise would never get the chance to know about golf," Mauro said.

Mauro also convinced Billy Andrade and Brad Faxon, the PGA tour stars to serve as honorary chairmen of the campaign. As they did in so many other areas, Andrade and Faxon not only allowed their names to be used, but became active backers of the course.

The project took a bit of a hit even as it was being built, through no fault of its own. A young couple out nightclubbing in Providence was kidnapped while in their own vehicle, driven to the gravel pit, and killed. The first time Button Hole made news was because an awful tragedy took place there.

It was not enough to stop the project. Once the ball got rolling, Mauro got more and more people involved, including state officials, led by Governor Lincoln Almond. Mauro kept providing us with more information, which he knew would help build more support. I was happy to provide the updates in the newspaper. It really was a wonderful idea. Much of the focus shifted to the fact that the goal was not merely to expose people to golf but also to teach them the life values that are such a big part of the game.

Button Hole opened in 2000. It is a nonprofit 501c3 initiative that is funded entirely by public donations. As its mission statement reads, "We are dedicated to providing a short course and teaching center focused on kids and 'golf, the greatest game.'" The mission is simple: "Enrich the lives of young people by providing facilities and programs that develop strong character, teach life values, and champion success through the game of golf."

Youngsters are allowed to use the facility for one dollar, although other arrangements can be made if they do not have the money. They become Button Hole Kids when they complete programs that teach not only about golf but about life and proper behavior. The state golf association moved its offices to Button Hole. The facility has a large driving range open to anyone and everyone, as the entire course is. Faxon and Andrade regularly offer clinics to the youngsters. Country clubs from around the state donate equipment that the children can use when they begin play at the course.

The facility already has produced on-course results. Two girls who learned the game there, Juliet Vongphoumy and Samantha Morrell, became the dominant girls' players in the state and earned college scholarships to Maryland and Old Dominion University (ODU), respectively, where both had terrific careers. Jamison Randall began as a Button Hole Kid before switching to full-sized courses. (Metacomet and Alpine Country Clubs both have offered support to Button Hole Kids). Randall also went to ODU, where he was the top player on the team. He turned pro when he graduated in 2015.

The work to keep the course alive and thriving goes on. It has become something of an inside joke among golfers who own businesses that they hide when they see Mauro because they know he will be asking for more support for Button Hole. The goal is to build an endowment that will make the facility self supporting.

It has worked out fabulously, and I do not feel at all guilty about pushing the idea to help it along. Eighteen thousand youngsters have become Button Hole Kids, and the facility continues to thrive.

Button Hole is not alone in providing community support through golf. Rhode Island also has one of the oldest scholarship programs in the country, the Burke Fund, which is celebrating its seventieth anniversary this year.

The Burke Fund began as a caddie scholarship program. It was named in honor of John P. Burke, the former state champion from Newport who was killed in World War II. Throughout the past seventy years, the program has awarded scholarships to more than 1,500 students and awarded more than $3 million in grants.

The organization has adapted with the changing times, to the point where it now accepts applications from anyone, male or female, who has worked for at least two years at the RIGA member course in any capacity, from the grounds crew to the dining room. The program is managed by Maury Davitt, and not only has survived through the years; it is now larger than ever. It awarded more than $144,000 in the past school year. I am proud to say I have played a tiny role as a member of the interview committee for the past two decades.

CHAPTER 20

THE PLAYOFFS

One of the many benefits of being the office utility man was having the opportunity to see the different ways each sport handles its championship competition.

As I look back on some of my souvenirs from the postseason events I covered, the thing that strikes me is how there really is no one way to do it. The methods are wildly different, which is good because the key is making the best use of the strengths of each sport. The common thread from where I saw it was that they all were fun to attend and handled well by the organizers.

As a reporter, the best part often was the lead-up, not the event itself. As I've stressed throughout here, for me the people involved make the events every bit as much as the contest itself. And we often learn more about the people before and after the game. The people include the fans that come to root for their teams.

Hockey fans from Wisconsin and North Dakota turned Providence into party city as they displayed their team colors when their schools took part in the NCAA Hockey Tournament at the Dunkin' Donuts Center, which is located next door to the *Journal* office in Providence. In the NCAA Basketball Tournament, seeing fans from eight different schools gather in Winston-Salem or Oklahoma City or wherever and put on displays to try to get their school noticed is a great show all by itself.

In Newport, when I covered the America's Cup early in my career, the city would get divided into bars and restaurants rooting for the Americans, while others were taken over by the visiting Australians. In Boston in April, when the Marathon is held, it is one big party at which everyone roots for everyone else. Runners speak about how spectators' incredible support helps them get through the 26.2 miles.

Watching a Stanley Cup playoff game from the ninth floor of the TD Garden in Boston offers a unique view, a chance to sense the speed and excitement of the game from a different perspective. It's a different feeling covering a Major League Baseball playoff game from the right-field stands, as is done in Yankee Stadium, or from the cafeteria, as is needed in tiny Fenway Park.

When someone asks what my favorite was, it is an easy response. It's not even close. The Super Bowl is an experience unlike any other.

Part of it is because of the situation. There is no moving from one city to another. It is a full week—eight or nine days, for a reporter—in one city with all activities planned and supervised by the NFL and with the host city putting its best foot forward to help make sure everyone has a good time.

I did two, Super Bowl XXXVI in New Orleans and Super Bowl XLVI in Indianapolis. The New Orleans game, when the Patriots shocked the Rams and the Greatest Show on Turf, was spectacular before, during, and after the game. Then again, the veteran Super Bowl reporters say the before and after was not a surprise, since New Orleans is the unquestioned top choice of location to hold the game by the people in the press box.

The Indianapolis game, where the Giants held off the Patriots, was almost as good. The people in Indianapolis did a sensational job in hosting the event, and they received a big boost when the weather turned out far better than expected.

The NFL has had major problems in recent years with the way it has handled off-field issues. Patriots fans, in particular, lost faith in the league with the way Tom Brady was treated in the Deflategate matter. But even New England fans would have to admit that when it comes to the Super Bowl, the NFL knows how to throw a party.

The biggest surprise for me when I covered my first Bowl in 2002 in New Orleans was how easy it was to work at the game. In fact, reporters receive so much help that it is one of the easiest weeks of the year, as far as gathering information. Players and coaches are more available that week than at any other time all season.

Everyone has seen the circus on the Tuesday of Super Bowl week, when every player and coach from both participating teams is made available, some with special stages of their own and others just sitting in the stands. There can be several hundred reporters trying to chase Tom Brady at the same time, while the backup offensive linemen sit and chat among themselves because no one wants to talk to them. The league opens that day to non-football media, so the appearance of, shall we say, unusual "reporters" dressed in costume or asking non-football questions, has become part of the show.

The other days of the week provide mass interviews with the head coaches and the team stars. What's more, each player must sit at a table in a different room and answer questions for forty-five minutes. It makes it tremendously easy to gather more than enough information to file reports. As if all that is not enough, the league has someone with recording devices at every press conference and with every player. The transcripts are compiled and made available for everyone. By the end of the week, there are long tables with quotes from just about everyone involved. On a typical day, a reporter might have time to interview five or six players personally, and ask questions he or she feels will help with the story. But there are quotes from fifty different players and coaches available within an hour or two of the press sessions.

I have two memories of my experiences at the Super Bowls that stand out. One was the opportunity to talk to Dante Scarnecchia, which I did at both games. Scarnecchia was the longest serving Patriots coach. He joined the team in 1982 when he came with head coach Ron Meyer to New England and spent all but two of the next thirty-two years with the Patriots working at various points as tight end coach, special teams coach, and most notably, as offensive line coach from 2000 until he retired in 2013. He has agreed to return in 2016. By the time he retired in 2013, Scarnecchia was the team's assistant head coach. In 1992, when then coach Dick McPherson became ill and missed the final eight games of the season, Scarnecchia took on the head coaching responsibilities.

Scarnecchia was as highly respected as anyone associated with the Patriots. I remember speaking with one of the team's locker room attendants one quiet day while waiting for players to return from practice, and Scarnecchia's name came up.

"He's the best. What a great guy," the worker said. He spoke about how good Scarnecchia was to work with every day and what Scarnecchia had done when he learned this attendant liked to surf.

"He has a place on the water, and he invited me there so I could surf. What a great day I had," he said.

There were numerous reports that Scarnecchia could have been a head coach. But he was not interested. He stayed with the Pats. He regularly would decline requests for interviews and speak only when required. Stacey James and Aaron Salkin, the Patriots' two public relations representatives, would tell everyone Scarnecchia was not being a problem; he simply did not care to speak.

When he had to speak at the Super Bowls, Scarnecchia was pleasant and cooperative, a complete gentleman. Asked why he did not like to speak, he said it simply was not for him. I found him a fascinating guy, a rarity in that he was satisfied to simply do his job. He did not care about seeking recognition.

The other major pre-game memory for me came in Indianapolis a decade later. It involved Marcus Cannon, an offensive lineman for the Patriots, and Mark Herzlich, a linebacker for the Giants. With a week to write stories about one game, it can be easy to get tired of writing about strategy or what one team was saying about the other. My penchant for being more interested in people led me to Herzlich and Cannon.

They were both young, part-time players on their teams, Herzlich from Boston College, Cannon from TCU. What they had in common was that they had made it to the NFL despite having cancer. Cannon was diagnosed as having non-Hodgkin's lymphoma. Herzlich suffered from a rare form of bone cancer in his left leg.

Early in the week, they were in demand, since their situations were so unusual. I waited until late in the week to talk to them, when there were fewer reporters chasing them. Both were outstanding in speaking about what they had gone through. Herzlich is an outgoing, talkative guy who speaks very well. Cannon is a shy, introverted person who seemed a bit uncomfortable with all the attention, but dealt with it nicely. The two related how their paths had crossed and they had become friends who helped each other battle their disease. I thought it ended up being the best story I did all week.

When work is finished at Super Bowl week, the NFL hosts all kinds of events to entertain media and fans. In New Orleans, there were parties that took over the mall near the Super Dome and entertainment in the French Quarter. In Indianapolis, the biggest party was at the Indianapolis Speedway, where food was available everywhere and a number of cars that take part in the Memorial Day 500 race were on display, complete with drivers and mechanics there to talk about their vehicles and the race.

Other championship events are far different. Early in my career, at both the America's Cup races in Newport and the Boston Marathon, I learned you don't really have to be at the event to report on it. In the boat race, only a select few reporters—those who know what they are watching—went on the press boat to see the race. Most of us sat in the Newport Armory on Thames Street, where we were told what had happened. We listened to the participants when they returned and wrote about what they said. At the Marathon, we received regular reports on who was ahead as we sat in a room in the John Hancock Building. The interviews with the winners were normal press conferences.

Baseball is different in the playoffs. In Yankee Stadium one year, my seat was deep in the right-field stands, while the interview and workrooms were in the cafeteria behind home plate. It is even more difficult at Fenway, where interviews are moved to a room behind the stands in left and the usual cafeteria becomes a workroom.

Hockey is similar. I saw the Bruins win the Stanley Cup by watching the first part of the game from a seat on the ninth floor, the main press area while action was going on. As the game was ending, many of us would head down to a section of the lobby, which was turned into a press area. We would sit at tables and watch the action on television.

Golf is actually easier at the majors than regular tour events because there is plenty of space to handle all the reporters and reporters are given badges to walk inside the ropes to follow the action. Golf, for what it's worth, became a way to measure the decline of newspapers as my career wound down. When Tiger Woods was dominating and the sport was exploding at the turn of the century, there would be three or four hundred reporters at Augusta or Pebble Beach or wherever the majors were held. By the time I finished, with the number of newspapers shrinking because of the Internet and social media, the number of reporters dropped in half, sometimes even more.

For sheer excitement, I felt the NCAA basketball and hockey tournaments were as much fun to cover as anything.

Lest I forget, the most unusual event I "covered" led me to interviewing a skateboarder. The X Games were held in Providence in 1996, showcasing skateboarding, motocross, BMX racing, and a variety of other events I knew nothing about. When I was assigned to do a feature, I did what I liked to do: found a participant who had an interesting back story and talked with him about his life, not so much his sport. I did the best I could to get out of there without embarrassing myself.

Early in his career, Paul Kenyon still had to comb his hair every day.

CHAPTER 21
WHERE DOES THE MONEY GO?

A sportswriter's work life is not complicated. Go to a game, tell everyone what happened, and then start all over again the next day. If there is no game, then it means go find someone who has an interesting story on whatever team you are covering and write about him or her.

That is what I did my entire career, with one exception. The exception turned into one of my most interesting experiences and one of the most rewarding, as well.

In 1995, our sports editors, Dave Bloss and Art Martone, asked me to do something different. I had begged off my assignment as one of the Red Sox beat writers three years earlier, and I had settled into my role as the office utility man, the one who did a little of everything. But I had never done anything like this.

In the 1990s, newspapers were still flourishing, staffs were sizeable, and the papers remained the prime source of information in the community. The *Journal* had a terrific investigative team that did marvelous work ferreting out and reporting on misdeeds by politicians and others. The sports department did not have anyone to do that on a regular basis. Bloss, the editor, wanted us to be involved on some level. In 1994 and into 1995, when baseball players went on strike, Bloss asked me to do an in-depth study of the relationship between athletes and agents.

This was at a time when there was labor turmoil in pro sports. There was no World Series in 1994. Replacement players were hired when there was still no agreement the next spring. The owners tried to impose a salary cap. Television networks were fighting over rights. More and more stories were exploding about athletes filing suit saying their agents had cheated them out of money. Bloss thought it was worth looking into.

"Let's study what happens to all the money athletes are making now," he said.

Salaries were exploding. Merchandising of sports gear was growing exponentially. More money than ever was being thrown around.

"Take some time to look into it. Find out all you can and see if we can do something about what's happening," Bloss said.

It was a dramatic change for me. I still did occasional daily work at a basketball game or a golf tournament, but for the most part, I spent several months researching, trying to learn as much as I could about the issue. It did not take long to realize this was a lot harder than the daily work, at least for me. I kept piling up more and more information. It really was a timely subject to investigate, because everything was in a dramatic state of change. But how was I to decide how to break down the different aspects?

As I wrote in the series, from the 1920s to the 1970s, the average salary for a professional athlete was only four or five times more than what the average working person made in the United States. When I did the series, the most recent figures available showed that the athletes were making thirty-four times more than the average worker.

That, of course, was just the beginning; everything has exploded even more since then. Salaries have gone from the hundreds of thousands into millions—and now, even hundreds of millions. I spoke with representatives of professional leagues, with agents and with as many athletes I could find who were willing to speak on the subject. The more I got into it, the more fascinated I became.

Rick Wise, who had an excellent career as a Major League pitcher, was the Pawtucket Red Sox pitching coach at the time. He was a big help in getting me started. He told me he had a net worth of $2.2 million when he retired as a player in 1982. Five years later, he found himself $800,000 in debt.

"I wasn't the one that did it. I wasn't the one who made the investments," he told me. "I trusted somebody else to do it, and he didn't do the job. It happened to me after my career was over. When the tax shelters were ruled against, I wasn't playing ball anymore. My top earning years were gone."

About the time I was conducting my study, a book was published on the subject, *An Athlete's Guide to Agents* by Bob Ruxin, then the vice president and general counsel of Kazmaier Associates Inc., a law firm in Concord, Massachusetts. It spoke about how unregulated the system was since the use of agents was still relatively new. Ruxin had strong views on the subject, opinions that many shared at that time.

"I think most agents are overpaid now," I quoted him as saying in one of the articles. "Four percent of such huge contracts is a lot of money. Bo Jackson's agent, who worked on an hourly basis, ended up being paid about 1 percent of his deal. You would expect there to be more price competition among agents, but I'm not sure that's happening."

It was an era when anyone could declare himself or herself an agent. There were 1,330 players in the NFL in the mid 1980s. At the same time, there were nearly two thousand agents registered to represent players. It was a terrible situation in many ways.

"There isn't a sports agent in the business who still has his soul," Mike Trope wrote in his book, *Necessary Roughness*. "Hell, they sold them to the devil years ago." Trope called agents "a lying pack of hypocrites."

Efforts to improve the situation were still in early stages.

Alex English, who had been a star in the NBA, was the director of player programs with the NBA Players Association. He was candid in speaking about the situation.

"We've all heard the horror stories. They've been documented," he said of players both wastefully spending money they made or being victimized by unscrupulous agents. "That's why we are working now on developing programs designed to eliminate a lot of the things we've heard about. It's an area we're focusing on."

Doug Allen, a former NFL linebacker who then was the assistant director of the NFL Players Association, also helped in the project.

"There are many instances where players have had long careers but then ended up with nothing to show for it," he told me. "There are all sorts of pressures today that we didn't face ten years ago. Now, with the money the players are getting coming out of college, the pressure is there immediately."

The biggest help of all, and the most impressive person of all to deal with, was Donald Fehr. He now is the executive director of the National Hockey League Players Association. But it was his work as executive director of the Major League Baseball Players Association that made him famous—and where he did the most good.

Fehr was going through a hectic time since he had led the players to their strike in August of the previous year. As it was, the baseball season was being reduced from 162 to 144 games in 1995 because of the labor trouble. Fehr was viewed as a villain in the matter in many quarters, being hailed as a hero by others.

I called his office in New York and explained what I was doing. I asked if it was possible to interview Fehr. To my delight, he got back to me and we set up an interview in his office in New York City. The trip was more than worth it. Fehr was outstanding.

The interview was different than most. When I was led into his office, he was disheveled and the place was a mess, boxes and books all over the place.

"We're in the process of moving," he said as he came over to shake hands. "Sorry about all this. I'm just going to kind of keep working on some of this as we talk, if you don't mind."

There was a chair for me to sit in so I was fine. I explained what I was doing and he clearly was happy to talk about the subject. He could not have been more helpful in explaining what the Players Association was doing to help its members deal with the rising problems. He told a story about how he had organized a program to educate the players on the matter a few years earlier.

"The players just weren't interested," he said. "There's this tendency to say, `Yeah, I know some planning should be done, some education has to be done, but it doesn't have to be done now. It can be done next year. It can be done the year after that because I'm going to be playing for however many more years.'

"I don't want to say it's a very serious problem in the sense that the country's going to collapse tomorrow if we don't do something about it," Fehr went on, "but it's one that affects lots and lots and lots of professional athletes."

Somewhere along the line, as we discussed the issue, he stopped rummaging through his books and papers and came over and sat on the couch next to me. He was a reporter's dream. I just pointed him in a direction, and he took off with pertinent, worthwhile information. Shortly before we finished, Mark Belanger, the former Orioles shortstop who was then one of Fehr's assistants, came in the room. When he saw me, he began to back away. Fehr told him to stay. He introduced me and told Belanger what I was doing. Belanger sat down and joined the conversion until, after about an hour, we finished. I used Fehr's words to sum up the situation in the lead article.

"The very people who are earning the money are the ones least prepared to handle it," Fehr said. "Five years ago, maybe five percent of the players were interested in financial and post-career programs organized by the union. Today maybe twenty-five percent."

The relationship between player and agent also was very much in flux, Fehr said. Programs designed to regulate agents were still being formulated.

"It's not a terribly tight program yet, but there's more and more interest from the players (in regulating agents). I think it's getting better, but slowly," Fehr offered. "If somebody asked me how good baseball agents are, that's not really a question I can answer. If you said `How is this agent?' That, I can answer."

"Obviously, one of the things anyone in our position would like to do in the long run is upgrade the level of service and reduce the fees," he went on. "But if you believe, as we do, that players ought to be able to essentially choose anyone they want and change their mind the way you or I do with a doctor or dentist, that's not easy to do. You have to allow for the reality that a statistical percentage of individuals in this group, like any others, will make decisions I would not recommend they make."

The series went on for four days, with two or three articles each day. I used basketball great Isaiah Thomas as an example of an athlete who was using his fame the right way, getting involved in established companies to make money beyond basketball. Baseball slugger Jack Clark, who had filed for bankruptcy two years after signing an $8.7 million contract, was the athlete I used as an example of someone who was handling his wealth in the wrong way.

As I look back at the stories, it is easy to see where steps were taken to try and better protect the athletes from themselves as time went on. Today, both the pro leagues and the unions offer educational programs that were not available twenty years ago. There are fewer horror stories of wasted riches, although they certainly have not gone away entirely.

In another of the articles in the series, I quoted Tom House, the former baseball pitcher, who I felt (and still feel) addressed the situation as well as anyone ever has. House had gone back to school and obtained a doctorate in psychology after his playing career. He knew about the problems. He filed personal bankruptcy after losing $1.1 million in a clothing and sporting goods business. He also later returned to the game as a pitching coach and an assistant general manager with the Texas Rangers. Most recently, House has been in the news for helping Patriots quarterback Tom Brady maintain his fitness as he gets older.

House speaks about how athletes are different. He calls it "terminal adolescence." He calls himself a confirmed terminal adolescent. He wrote a book about it, *The Jock's Itch*, published in 1989.

"With athletes, because they are special people with special genetic talents, they are not asked to perform the tasks others are expected to," he wrote. "A normal individual, as he progresses, is asked to become a brother, a friend, a classmate. An athlete is treated differently. He is told he is special. He is told he doesn't have to do the things that are expected of everyone else."

"There is a traveling secretary to take care of travel arrangements; there is the clubhouse guy to take care of clothes and cleaning and to run errands. There are agents to take care of financial and family planning. The athlete is not expected, nor asked, to perform real-life skills," House wrote.

There are times when I'm not happy when I look back on work I've done. But I must say that reviewing that series is a pleasant experience. I was not thrilled when I was asked to do it, because it was not something I felt comfortable doing. But I thank Dave Bloss and Art Martone for having me do it.

I'm also happy when I look at the wall in my office at home. There is a nice plaque with the Associated Press emblem at the top that reads: "New England Associated Press, News Executive Association, sports story, first place, Paul Kenyon, Providence Journal-Bulletin."

Press passes these days are much slicker than they used to be.

CHAPTER 22

HIGH SCHOOL

Before I began covering college basketball, before I began chasing pro athletes, my first work in athletics was with the high schools.

It is how I began fifty-two years ago while I was a student at Bishop Hendricken High. From my sophomore year on, I wrote about the basketball, baseball, and football teams for the *Pawtuxet Valley Daily Times*, the local paper three blocks from my home. I learned much from Amby Smith, the great sports editor there who took me under his wing and provided wonderful guidance. When I began college at URI, I stayed on with the paper working weekends through my time in college.

My inclination back then was to work in sports. Growing up in West Warwick meant my life revolved around sports. Some of my first memories are going to West Warwick High games at the old Athletic Field, which was adjacent to the town dump, and watching the great Monk Maznicki-coached teams win one football and baseball championship after another.

It was Mr. Smith who helped get me involved in writing for newspapers. I loved it from the start, to the point where my big Christmas present my junior year in high school was a Smith-Corona typewriter that I still have to this day. I would go the games, return home, type up a story, and walk the three blocks from my home to drop it off for Mr. Smith.

In college, my mentor was Professor Wilbur Doctor, who became one of the greatest influences in my life. It was a two-man Journalism Department at URI, and Doctor taught all the practical courses. He was a former *Providence Journal* writer and editor. He was a fabulous teacher. He also was anti-sports. This was the late 1960s, when student protests over Vietnam were dominating college campuses. Real-life concerns hit everyone in the face. Sports fell more into the background for many of us.

By the time I graduated, Doctor had convinced me to go into news reporting, not sportswriting.

"You've got too much ability to waste it in the sports department," he told me at one of the many sessions we had to discuss my work. I was flattered and honored. By that time, he was one of the most important people in my life.

Professor Doctor even got me my first job. One day late in my senior year, after I had already begun interviewing for potential jobs, he called me into his office. As usual, he went right to the point.

"You have a job yet?" he asked.

"No. I've got a couple things on the line, but nothing set," I told him.

"You want a job? I've got one for you. It will be good for you," he said. "It's the *Pawtucket Times*, a news reporter."

"Wow. I don't know. One of the things I'm involved in is with the *Providence Journal*. They came here for interviews a couple weeks ago, and I received a letter last week inviting me to go to the *Journal* for a second interview," I explained.

"Ahhh, take the one in Pawtucket. It's a smaller paper, and a good one. You will get to do more there right away and, if you're as good as I think you are, you will get a job at the *Journal* later on and be better off for it," he said.

While I was in the office, he picked up the phone and called Ves Sprague, then the executive editor of the Pawtucket paper, and told him I was sitting in the office and ready to go to Pawtucket for an interview.

"He's the guy you want," I heard him tell Sprague.

So, the next week—remember, we were still in school—I drove to Pawtucket. When I walked into Sprague's office, he stood up, shook my hand, and, as we were sitting down, said, "When can you start?"

I was stunned. There were no questions. He had not even looked at my resume.

"If Wilbur says you're the guy I want, that's good enough for me," Sprague said.

I fumbled a bit and told him I was waiting to hear on other possibilities so I was not ready to agree to anything. He said he would give me one week to decide. If he did not hear from me by then, he would get someone else. The whole session lasted perhaps five minutes.

When I went back to campus, I told Doctor what had happened.

"Take the job," he said firmly. "It's right for you."

So I did. I began working in Pawtucket a week before graduation ceremonies. I spent four years as the utility guy on the ten-reporter news staff. When Dave Chmielewski, the police reporter, needed help or went on vacation, I helped with police and fire coverage. When Tom Izzo, the Central Falls reporter, was away, I covered Central Falls. When Ed Murphy, the city hall guy, was out, I covered district court and the mayor's office.

When nothing was happening, I was in the office, taking obituaries, writing features on fiftieth wedding anniversary stories and doing a little of everything.

It was great training. The people were terrific. The opportunities to learn and do different things were everywhere. The preparation I had been given by Professor Doctor turned out to be ideal. I loved the job.

Four years in, I was asked to change. Jim Murphy, one of the greatest newspaper people I ever worked for, had taken over as executive editor after Mr. Sprague retired. He called me into his office one day and began chatting about sports. Jim was a big sports guy and was especially a fan of baseball. He had been one of the prime movers in bringing pro baseball to McCoy Stadium, first as a farm team of the Indians and later, of course, as the Red Sox Triple-A team.

After we talked about Chico Walker or Chris Coletta or one of the other guys then playing for Pawtucket, Jim asked if I would be interested in switching to the sports department.

Sports was a two-man operation, with Ted Mulcahey and Paul Calderone. Jim knew that I enjoyed sports and that I had done some sportswriting for Amby Smith at the *Pawtuxet Valley Daily Times*. He said Paul Calderone was going to move to the news department, and I was the obvious choice to take his spot helping Ted in sports.

I hesitated. I liked what I was doing. But spending the day going to ball games was just too good to pass up. I agreed to the move.

I spent the next three years covering sports in the Blackstone Valley. Ninety percent of the job was writing about the dozen high schools in the region covered by the *Times*. It did not take long for me to reach a conclusion. As much as I enjoyed the news side, there was no doubt this was even better. This was me.

I got to know and work with the coaches and athletes from Cumberland, Lincoln, Central Falls, all the Pawtucket schools, and Seekonk, Attleboro, North Attleboro, and Bishop Feehan, too. One of the first things to strike me was how many terrific people were involved in helping make for a great atmosphere in the high school leagues.

By this time, the craziness of the 1960s was gone, and stability reigned. School sports were exploding, becoming bigger than ever in high school. The soccer boom was underway and seemed to be getting bigger every year. Lacrosse was just beginning, and, most of all, girls' programs were arriving, big time.

This was before television and before cable, never mind the Internet. High school sports were still a main source of entertainment, especially in the smaller towns where the teams had a history of success.

Most of the coaches were still teachers, trained educators who knew not only how to put together a team but also how to help teenagers learn right from wrong. The Blackstone Valley was loaded with teacher/coaches who did outstanding jobs on and off the field. Tolman had one of the all-time great staffs, which included Gig and Rollie Pariseau in football, Jim Donaldson Sr. in basketball, and Ted McConnon in baseball. Every school had special coaches, like Denny O'Brien at St. Raphael; Frank Geiselman, Steve Gordon, and Tom Kenwood at Cumberland; Howie Catley, Cathy Tiberii, and John Rekos at Lincoln; and Roger Berard, Tony Rainone, and Mike Goodson at Central Falls.

Soon, I was to learn that the Blackstone Valley schools were not alone. Every school, it seemed, was fortunate to have teachers who also were terrific coaches.

While most of the work with the *Times* revolved around high schools, summers brought a change. By then, I had developed a liking for golf, so I volunteered to cover some of the Rhode Island Golf Association events, especially anything held in the Valley. While doing that, I met the golf writer from the *Providence Journal*, Ed Duckworth, who also was the paper's assistant sports editor.

It did not take long for me to begin enjoying time with Duckworth, who was and is one of the great characters in the business. He would have his ever-present cigar in his mouth and would complain about anything and everything and tell everyone he would not be happy until he could get to a racetrack so he could bet the horses. He did all he could to make everyone think he was an irritable, unhappy human being. The truth was, it was all an act.

He was a terrific newspaperman who went out of his way to help new guys on the scene, like me. He ended up helping change my life. In the summer of 1977, I made the one and only job change in my career because of Duckworth and Gene Buonaccorsi, the *Journal's* sports editor.

I arrived home from the office one evening, rushing a bit because my wife, Pauline, was overdue with what would be our second child, Jayson. It was hot and, being nine months pregnant, Pauline was a bit irritable.

"How you feeling?" I asked. "Anything happening?"

"No. I feel awful. Nothing. I'm so hot," she shot back. Then, seconds later, she added, "There was a telephone call for you. I wrote down his name and number. He said he wanted you to call him as soon as possible."

I looked at the note. The spelling was not good, but close enough that I recognized it.

"That's Gene Buonaccorsi, the sports editor at the *Journal*," I told Pauline. "Why's he calling me here? Why didn't he just call me at the office?"

She did not know and, right about then, did not care. Once I got squared away, I called the number, which was Mr. Buonaccorsi's home phone. The call was one of the most important of my life. He made a few pleasantries, introduced himself a bit since we barely knew each other, and then got to the point.

"Dick Reynolds is retiring," he said. "We need someone to replace him. Your name has come up. Are you interested?"

Dick Reynolds was the *Journal's* legendary high school sports editor. Like every other kid in Rhode Island, I grew up reading his reports on Rhode Island high school sports. He wrote for the paper for more than forty years. He also was a prominent after-dinner speaker at sports dinners, a terrific entertainer with a dry, low-key sense of humor.

"Sure, yes, of course I'd be interested, Mr. Buonaccorsi," I responded.

"I'd like to speak to you as soon as I can," he said. "Can we meet for lunch one day this week?"

"You tell me the day," I responded, doing what I could to keep my enthusiasm in check. A couple days later, we met at a restaurant near the airport in Warwick. We chatted a bit as we ordered and then he got down to business. It turned out to be Ves Sprague revisited.

"When can you start?" he said.

I was a bit flustered.

"Start?" I repeated.

"Yes. We need to do a bunch of things to get you hired, and it's getting close to the start of school. We have to get you in as fast as we can."

It was the second, and to be the final, job of my career. Like the first, I never filled out a job application. I had only one hesitation, so I asked Mr. Buonaccorsi if I could have twenty-four hours to think about it.

I went home and told Pauline what had happened. Ted Mulcahey, my sports editor at the *Times*, was getting old and was likely to retire soon, although as it turned out, he died several years later after becoming ill following a Patriots game. I knew I was in line to be my own boss if I stayed. Of course, *Pawtucket* was about 20 percent the size of the *Journal*, not in the same league in many areas, including salary.

"Will you make more money if you take the job in Providence?" Pauline asked. When I told her yes, I was not sure how much but it definitely was more, she did not hesitate.

"How can you even think about not taking it? It's the *Providence Journal*," she said.

She was right, of course, as usual. I called Mr. Buonaccorsi that night, accepted the job, and asked what I had to do. I made two trips to the *Journal* office to speak to the necessary people and fill out forms. I told everyone involved that if they could not reach me, it would be because we would be at the hospital having a baby.

On August 12, Mr. Buonaccorsi woke me with an early-morning call.

"I was trying to reach you yesterday. I assume you were at the hospital. Did you have a boy or a girl?" was the way he began the conversation. I was happy to tell him it was a boy, and he was getting the name of a *Journal* sportswriter.

Pauline is not a sports fan. It is one reason we never had office issues when I came home. She does not care about any sport. But in the two weeks between the first call from Mr. Buonaccorsi and the baby's birth, she had begun reading the *Journal* sports page. The rising young star at the time was Jayson Stark, who went on to a great career in Philadelphia and ESPN. She liked the name Jayson. She had advocated for it during the pregnancy, but I talked her out of it. It was going to be Andrew George after our two fathers.

I helped coach her at the birth and enjoyed the most memorable day of my life. Being there, helping coach, and seeing the birth is the single greatest experience a man can have. It was truly wonderful. The doctor never had to hit him on the bottom. Jayson started crying the second he was born.

Minutes later, as Pauline was recovering, we enjoyed a time of true joy. Then she looked up and with her first words asked, "Can we name him Jayson?"

It was a rigged situation, and she knew it. There was no way any father could say no after seeing what she had just gone through. So he is Jayson Paul.

The next day, after getting the call from Mr. Buonaccorsi, I went to the *Times*, typed a two-paragraph letter of resignation, said thank you to the many good friends I had made, and then went straight to the *Journal* and signed papers. I had a new job.

It was much the same except that I was covering fifty schools, instead of twelve. And it was much nicer on payday.

Instead of being on my own, there was plenty of help. John Gillooly, who already had been there as a part-time guy for some time (he also worked at Bryant College) helped ease me into the system. He was a great working partner for the next eleven years. Larry

Gallogly and Bill Troberman were older guys who took many of the calls reporting scores. Like John, they were walking history books on the Interscholastic League. Bobby McGarry, who for many of us was the office MVP, did all the little things to make everything work.

At one point, when the paper decided to publish special sections for each part of the state, we had as many as eight people covering the high schools. Bob Dick, Bob Leddy, Al Aleixo and Bud Barker had their areas. Carolyn Thornton, a former All-State softball player herself and then all-Ivy at Brown, joined our team. Jimmy Salisbury and Joe McDonald, both of whom have gone on to terrific careers in other, bigger markets, got started with us and made it clear early on they were big-time talents, not to mention terrific guys to work with.

Everything worked well. The only difficult part was picking the All-State teams. As I knew, it meant a lot to be a *Journal* All-Stater. Coaches often pushed for their athletes. The bad news was that space was extremely limited. Mr. Buonaccorsi, the old-fashioned, strait-laced guy that he was, never allowed the changes that are in place now.

It was not a matter of picking the twenty-one or twenty-five or twenty-eight best football players, which might include five quarterbacks and no tackles, as is done now. The rules then were strict. A team was a real team. There had to be one quarterback, one center, and two guards in football. In baseball, there could not be four shortstops and no second baseman, as is allowed these days. There had to be one shortstop and one of everything.

I learned quickly how much it mattered. I received calls from parents and grandparents saying I had ruined their child or grandchild's life by not selecting him or her for the team. One year, when the soccer team roster was released, someone called in a death threat to the office, and I had to meet with the state police to make them aware of what had happened.

It was suggested that I should get an unlisted phone number, because some of the calls would go to my home. I never did that, because I've always felt that it was better to speak to all callers rather than try and hide from them. It was my experience then, and still is, that talking things out helps everyone involved, although there are times when it can make for difficult situations.

One year at the dinner held for the All-State football team, one coach who was upset that one of his players had not been selected had a bit too much to drink. As a number of us were chatting after the dinner, he came past and started yelling at me, with a few curse words thrown in. Thankfully, a couple of the other coaches stepped in and pulled him away before it became a real problem.

If there was one area that I feel most proud about in the eleven years I covered the high schools for the *Journal*, it was that we did more than had ever been done to get as many names in the paper as possible. We ran the Stars of the Week, in which would recognize two, three, even five athletes from every sport for doing something special the previous week.

Also, at my request, we cut back a bit on game coverage to allow for more feature stories. My tendency for preferring stories about people more than about games was brought forth again. Obviously, reporting the winner of each game is important. But judging from the reaction I received about stories featuring kids who overcame adversity, who excelled in areas beyond sports, or who were excellent students, were far better read. So, we ran features on people as often as possible. With fifty schools and nearly twenty different sports, there was a never-ending pool of material.

As I had learned in Pawtucket, the vast majority of coaches were great to work with. They helped create what was a smooth-functioning league. I should not leave any discussion of the league without mention of the people in charge.

The Principals' Committee on Athletics is the governing body. As the name implies, it is made up of school principals who give of their time to provide guidance for everyone. The people in charge were truly special, most notably the Rev. Robert C. Newbold, and later Dick Lynch, for the boys' programs, and Alice Sullivan for the girls'.

Sullivan, a teacher at East Providence High, will go down as one of the most important people ever in athletics in the state. She became involved at a time when girls were still fighting to be afforded the same opportunities as the boys. Sullivan became a tireless campaigner for the girls as well as a tremendous administrator for their programs. She was one truly special person and educator.

CHAPTER 23

ONE-TIMERS

I had plenty of unusual assignments, one-time experiences. Almost without exception, they were fun. They fit into my love of doing something different, meeting new people, and seeing how events are run.

One of the most memorable involved the highly unlikely trio of Gene Buonaccorsi, Vinny Pazienza, and John Denver.

Buonaccorsi was the long-time sports editor at the *Journal*, the man who hired me. His way of doing things was calm and under control at all times. He liked to smoke a pipe as he made plans and discussed assignments with Ed Duckworth, who was his assistant and a very different type of guy. Duckworth liked to act like a tough guy as he kept a cigar butt in his mouth, but he actually was a funny guy and a good man.

One day in the fall of 1993, as I was doing some college basketball prep work in the office, they called me over. As I headed toward them, I saw Duckworth with a smirk on his face, a bit of a warning that this would be something different.

"We were just looking at the schedule," Buonaccorsi began, "and thinking about that fight Pazienza has in Colorado over Christmas."

I had covered a couple Pazienza matches when he was early on his road to being a world-class boxer, but Duckworth was our boxing guy. He did most of the Pazienza fights and whatever other boxing news needed to be covered. I looked at him when Buonaccorsi brought up Pazienza. He was still smiling.

"We were just thinking that as long as you are going to be out there, it would be easier if you just did the boxing and the basketball tournament," the boss said.

"Out there" was Kansas City. URI was going to play in the Great Harvest Classic in Kansas City on December 28. I stood there drawing a picture in my mind of where Kansas City was and where Aspen was. They were not exactly next door. I looked it up later. They are almost eight hundred miles apart.

I looked at Duckworth. He made no effort to stop smiling. He made it clear he was not interested in spending part of the holiday season in the Rocky Mountains. So it was that I received what turned out to be one of the truly memorable assignments of my life. I was able to spend Christmas with my family, but left the next day to fly to Aspen for the Pazienza match on December 27. Pazienza was to fight Dan Sherry, a journeyman near the end of his career. Pazienza always has loved publicity—they have made a movie of his life—and the goal was to attract the celebrity crowd that dominates the Aspen scene.

Aspen was different in many ways. It was cheaper to stay for two days in an apartment than a hotel. The area was simply beautiful and, with Christmas decorations up, the whole place looked like a movie set. The fight was in the ballroom of the Ritz Carlton Hotel. The crowd was disappointing, as only a couple hundred showed up. Ivana Trump, who had just gotten divorced from Donald, made a grand entrance and added some life, but otherwise, it was very sedate, especially for a boxing match. Just before the fight began, two people came to sit in the small area set up for reporters. They sat directly behind me. I did a double take when I turned and looked at them.

It was John Denver, the singer, and LeRoy Neiman, the artist with the big handlebar moustache who did a lot of work involving sports. They smiled and said hello.

As the fight went on, it was obvious Pazienza was in control. He knocked out Sherry in the eleventh round, which meant it was time for me to get to my serious work. It was late evening, midnight back home. I already had missed deadlines for the early editions. In 1993, there was no Internet. We had bigger, more cumbersome machines to use to file our stories. The press room organizers had set up was around the corner from the ballroom where the fight was held. The computer had to be left there. The closest telephone also was in that room. I was torn on whether to run to the other room and call in a few graphs about what had happened to make as many editions as I could or wait to speak to Pazienza. I started to leave the room but then stopped, and I guess I made it obvious I was unsure what to do.

"You need help?" Denver asked.

I turned, told him I was on deadline and was not sure what to do. He volunteered to help. He said he would tell me if anything happened in the ring and would make sure Pazienza did not get away. (There were only two other reporters there to cover the fight.)

I accepted his offer, ran to the other room, used the phone to dictate the basics of what had happened to the office, and then ran back. Denver assured me nothing significant had happened. I thanked him for his help and went about doing my job from there.

The next morning, it was on to Kansas City, where URI gave Kansas a solid test before the Jayhawks, then the fifth-ranked team in the country, won 73–60.

Combining two assignments in one was fairly commonplace for us. Another similar trip also involved URI basketball.

The Rams arranged a game at the University of Florida against Billy Donovan's Gators, then one of the national powers. One of Rhode Island's top athletes, swimmer Elizabeth Beisel, was excelling at Florida. The North Kingstown grad had earned an Olympic bronze medal and was winning NCAA titles for Florida in the backstroke and individual medley.

So, on the day of the basketball game, the Florida sports information department helped arrange an interview with Beisel after practice at the beautiful aquatic center on campus. Beisel was terrific as she spoke about how happy she was with college life, about how nice it was to wake up every morning and look out at palm trees rather than snow, and how great the swim program was at her school.

I went from there to get ready for the basketball game, wrote about how URI could not handle the Gators in hoops, and then, on the way home, did a feature that ran a couple days later on how well Beisel was doing in Gainesville.

Doing one-time events did not pertain only to the trips involved, but also the people involved. Very early in my career, I had the chance to spend a day with Sam Snead and another with Ted Williams. It meant a lot, since both were among the greats in American sports history. Nearly forty years later, as I think about it now, it means even more.

Williams and Snead were both in their sixties when I met them, both already part of American sports lore. Both were very different by then, not the sometimes difficult to work with characters they were in their prime. They were pleasant grandfather types who were just trying to enjoy themselves.

Snead came to Newport to compete in the Merrill Lynch/Golf Digest Golf Tournament, an event that was the predecessor to what is now the Champions Tour. Rhode Island's Stan Abrams, a former Harvard athlete and a two-time Rhode Island Amateur Golf champion and RIGA Hall of Famer, was among the first to organize the older players, so Rhode Island was a natural place for such an event. Newport, of course, was the site of both the first US Open and US Amateur.

Snead, then sixty-eight years old, shot his age, going 69–67 to win the thirty-six-hole event. It turned out to be the last individual victory of his career.

Williams came to East Greenwich, Rhode Island, to help dedicate a new baseball field that friends of his, the Briggs family, had built. He no longer was the Splendid Splinter I had watched as I was growing up. I had read many times about how much trouble he had getting along with reporters in his prime. By the time I met him, he could not have been any nicer, a sweet, gentle older man who patiently answered questions from this young reporter. It was a great experience.

One of my first assignments out of state came in 1980 when Pawtucket's Little League team won the Northeast Championship and earned a trip to the Little League World Series in Williamsport, Pennsylvania.

Dealing with the twelve-year-olds was flat-out fun. It was made even better by the fact that George Patrick Duffy, a legend in Rhode Island as a broadcaster and publicist, was the coach. The team lost to Tampa, Florida, a squad led by Gary Sheffield who went on the Major League stardom, in the first round, and then won twice in the losers bracket before being eliminated.

As I looked back on that trip, the names come back, kids like Billy Karalis, Brian Daily, John Bradley, and Paul Coutu. Duffy told a story about what the experience was like for the players. He said that after the loss to Tampa, he was debating how he would speak to his players to cheer them up. It turned out he did not have to worry about it.

"When I was going back to the dorms, I heard this noise. The kids were already in the swimming pool playing and laughing," Duffy said. "They had forgotten already."

As far as I can recall, I had only one face-to-face meeting with Harry Sinden, the longtime Boston Bruins coach and general manager. It only lasted seconds, but it almost got me in trouble.

It was in Greensboro, North Carolina, in April of 1999 in a playoff against Carolina. The Hurricanes had moved south from Hartford, where they were the Whalers, but the rink that was to become their home in Raleigh was not ready, so the team played the season in Greensboro. We did not have a regular hockey writer at the time, so I was assigned to cover the games in Greensboro.

While we were there, my computer broke. I went to two computer stores on the day of the game, but neither could determine what was wrong. So that night, I dictated my stories by telephone. I gave updates after each period by going from the press box at the top of the stands down to the press room on the bottom floor. The Bruins were ahead, 3–2, with about four or five minutes left, so I decided to head down the stairs and begin dictating a story from the press room as I watched the end on television.

As I headed down from one direction, there came Sinden heading down from the opposite side. As we neared the bottom, I turned to Sinden and started to say, "Congratulations, Harry, that's a—"

I was going to congratulate him on a big victory. But I never got to finish it. Sinden, like so many other coaches and athletes, was superstitious. The game was not done. He did not want to hear about winning and going ahead, 3–2, in the series.

"Don't say it," he said. So I stopped. I never finished the sentence.

About ten seconds later, just after we had reached the bottom and gone in different directions, a huge roar came up. Carolina had scored and tied the game. I turned around and was happy to see that Sinden was out of sight. The good news for Sinden was that about two hours later, in double overtime, the Bruins did win.

Finally, I have one other one-time story, perhaps the most blatant as to why I enjoyed my job so much. This one involved spending a day at the racetrack.

In 1990, simulcast wagering came to Rhode Island. It is now commonplace to be able to bet on horse and dog racing at home, never mind the nearest racetrack. Back then, though, it was a breakthrough to be able to bet on races being held in other states.

Rhode Island long has had a history with gambling. There were two racetracks in the state as I was growing up, Narragansett Park in Pawtucket and Lincoln Downs. Like so many others, I read about the races in the *Journal* and began visiting the tracks when I was old enough. I enjoyed it then and still enjoy it now.

It led to another one of my ideas. I suggested that it would be fun to bet on tracks from around the country and then write about it to tell everyone about what was now available. I did not have to work hard to sell it. I received approval and $200 to spend. I decided to get as much out of it as I could.

By 1990, the horses were long gone, and the simulcasting was held at what had become Lincoln Greyhound Park, built on the same property as the old horse track. (It has since turned into the Twin River Casino.)

I went early and stayed late. I "worked" for more than eleven hours (and that did not include the time needed to write the story after it was finished). I bet on eighty-one races at tracks in six states. I bet on horse racing, greyhound racing, and harness racing, as well as both the afternoon and evening dog racing cards at Lincoln. Ed Duckworth, the biggest horse-racing guy in the office, provided guidance, and so did Scott Pianowski, the sports department's most regular visitor to the dog races. Those two guys lasted about six hours before telling me I was on my own.

We bet win, place, and show, exactas, trifectas, and eight different daily doubles, and even won two of the doubles. Obviously, we were not betting big money. We bet a total of $189. We won $167.20, for a net loss of $21.80. That did not include $3 for seating, $11.50 for programs and $24.50 for meals (yes, the *Journal* paid for all of that, too).

It was just another day at the office, a tough job but, hey, someone had to do it. I was glad it was me.

Providence College coach Dave Gavitt works with
Marvin Barnes, one of his greatest players.

CHAPTER 24

THE TWENTIETH CENTURY

There were times when I talked myself into some serious work. One came at the turn of the century.

Many outlets did stories—most of them on the news side—about the movers and shakers in the twentieth century, people who made the biggest impacts. Naturally, some of us spoke about how we should do something like that involving sports in Rhode Island. Not surprisingly, considering my role in the department, I volunteered to see what we could do.

I knew it was a no-win project. No matter the subject, those types of lists draw more criticism than praise. It's human nature. Everyone has his or her opinion.

But that type of list does draw a lot of interest. It is fun to discuss and debate. I also found it fun to do. It was an interesting change. I ended up compiling a list of the fifty most influential people in sports in the state in the twentieth century.

The criteria was for general impact, not necessarily simply for how good the athlete or coach was. Another aspect was how involved the person was in the state. More credit was given to someone who lived in Rhode Island than someone who then left and did his or her work elsewhere. Another complicating factor was how to compare an athlete as opposed to a coach or administrator.

If there was a trend, I discovered, it was that Rhode Island produced an abnormally high number people who made impacts as a coach or administrator. As I look at it with the benefit of hindsight, I see a number of places where I would rank people differently if I were doing it today. And I can think of a number of people who were not included but should have been, like Jeremy Kapstein and Roland Hemond from baseball, marathon runner Bobby Doyle, and high school coaches Jack Cronin, Gail Davis, and John Toppa.

This is the list I came up with, as published in the *Journal*. The bios are updated:

1. **Dave Gavitt**

   I spoke in the basketball section about my admiration for Gavitt. He was special in so many areas. Even today, the benefits of his work are still being enjoyed, including the Dunkin' Donuts Center. There is no way that facility would have been built without Providence College basketball. Gavitt was the best, simply the most talented person I ever had the pleasure top work with.

2. **Ben Mondor**

   As I related in the baseball section, Mondor was the most beloved man in Rhode Island by the time he ended his work with the Pawtucket Red Sox.

   He became more than the owner of a baseball team. He treated fans as if they were all his children, welcoming them to the park, walking through the stands, and working to keep prices down. He put together a dedicated staff. Beyond that, he got the team, and the players, involved in the community, especially in charitable causes. He stood for going about your work the right way.

3. Napoleon Lajoie

Rhode Island does not produce many Hall of Famers in the major sports, but it had one in Woonsocket's Lajoie. He was one of the first Major League stars of the twentieth century.

He played from 1896 to 1916 and managed the Cleveland Naps while he was playing from 1905–09. He led the American League in hitting five times, finished with 3,252 hits and a career average of .339. In 1901, he set the American League record for highest batting average ever, at .426, a mark that still stands.

4. Glenna Collett Vare

Another Hall of Famer in her sport, golf, she was one of the country's first great female players.

She accomplished so much that the trophy for lowest scoring average on the LPGA Tour is named after her, as is the trophy for the winner of the USGA Girls' Championship, a trophy Vare donated herself.

She was introduced to golf at age nine by her father, George, who was one of the founding members at Metacomet in East Providence. She won six US Women's Amateur Championships between 1922 and 1935, a record that has never been matched among men or women. She was among six charter members of the Women's Golf Hall of Fame.

5. Joe Mullaney

A native New Yorker, he came to New England to play basketball in the 1940s at Holy Cross, where he was one of the starters on the 1947 squad that won the national championship.

He played briefly as a pro for the Boston Celtics in 1949–50, and then began a career with the FBI. That was brief because he decided he wanted to get into coaching. He spent one year at Norwich in Vermont and was hired by Providence College in 1955. He is the man who turned the Friar program from a regional one into a national one.

He won 319 games in eighteen seasons at PC, with 164 losses. His teams won the NIT in both 1960 and 1961.

He left Providence when wooed by the pros, spent time coaching the Los Angeles Lakers and later in the ABA, where he was coach of the year in 1974 with the Utah Stars. His Kentucky Colonels team in the ABA went 68–16 in 1971–72, the best record ever in that league. He finished his career back home in the college ranks with Brown and PC.

6. Frank Keaney

He was the first great basketball coach in the state, doing so at URI, where he also taught chemistry.

His plaque in the Basketball Hall of Fame, where he was inducted in 1960, describes what he did very nicely: "Known as the architect of the modern run-and-shoot basketball, Frank Keaney's uptempo style made use of a fast-breaking offense and a full-court defense. Keaney's innovative tactics enabled his 1939 Rhode Island club to become the first college team to score better than 50 points per game.

In 1943, Rhode Island averaged over two points per minute (80.7) earning them the nickname, 'The Firehouse Gang.' In 27 seasons at Rhode Island, Keaney had only one losing season and led the Rams to four NIT appearances. When Keaney decided to enter the professional leagues, he became the first coach ever to be signed by the Boston Celtics. He was unable to take the position because of health reasons."

He finished his career as URI athletic director.

7. Brad Faxon

The Barrington product has been one of the most visible athletes in Rhode Island for the past forty years, in part because even as he played on the PGA Tour, he kept Rhode Island as his home base for most of his career. He served as an active and very visible member of the community.

Faxon was among the last young golfers to play most of his junior tournaments at home, rather than on the national circuit that is so prevalent now. He won three Rhode Island Junior Championships and the state and New England Amateur titles.

He attended Furman, where he was a two-time All-American, the college player of the year, and a member of the Walker Cup team. When he turned pro, he earned a spot on the PGA Tour, where he won eight events, played on two Ryder Cup teams, and earned more than $17 million.

He now plays on the Champions Tour, although he is limited because he also is a member of the Fox telecast team, which now has the contract for all USGA events.

Off the course, Faxon has been heavily involved in charitable work both through the CVS Charity Classic he and Billy Andrade co-host and the Andrade-Faxon Children's Charities program. Between them, the two programs have raised more than $24 million for area charities.

8. Davey Lopes

No Rhode Islander has spent as much time in a Major League Baseball uniform as Lopes. The East Providence native, who went to La Salle Academy, had a rare combination of power and speed, especially for a second baseman.

A second-round draft choice of the Dodgers, he played fifteen years in the majors for four teams, most notably Los Angeles, where he spent his first nine years. He was one of the best leadoff hitters in the game for years. He had 557 career stolen bases, and his success rate of 83.1 percent is third best in history. In 1975, he broke the Major League record with thirty-eight consecutive stolen bases without being caught.

But he also had power, belting 155 home runs, including twenty-eight in 1979. He made the All-Star team four years in a row, beginning in 1978, in six National League Championship Series and four World Series, highlighted by winning the title in 1981. He had three home runs and seven RBI in the 1987 series against the Yankees.

When he finished playing, he became a coach. He worked for six different teams and is still the first-base coach for the Dodgers. Milwaukee hired him as manager in 2000, and he compiled a 144–195 record before being fired in 2002.

One of Providence's largest recreation centers is named in his honor.

9. Billy Andrade

The Bristol native has been a success in almost everything he has touched since he was a teenager, on and off the golf course.

He led his Bristol Little League team to the state championship as a twelve-year-old. He was a prep All-State basketball player at Providence Country Day School. Most of his life, though, has been devoted to golf. He became a national figure when he twice won the Insurance Youth Classic, then the biggest junior tournament in the country. He accepted the Arnold Palmer Scholarship to Wake Forest, where he helped the Demon Deacons win a national championship.

He represented the United States in the Junior World Cup and won major amateur events, including the North and

South and the Sunnehanna. He also was a member of the Walker Cup team.

When he turned pro, he jumped straight to the PGA Tour, where he won more than $12 million, and he is now a leading player on the Champions Tour.

As much money as he has earned on the course, he has helped raise even more in his charitable work with good friend Brad Faxon. The two have raised more than $17 million through the CVS Classic and another $7 million in their own Children's Charities program.

10. Ernie Calverley

Few Rhode Islanders ever have been more closely associated with the state university than Calverley. The Pawtucket native spent virtually his entire adult life working for the school. That came after becoming one of the greatest basketball players in school history.

Calverley excelled at Pawtucket High School (now Tolman) and then headed to URI, where he scored 1,868 points from 1943–46 in the new fast-break offense launched by Coach Frank Keaney. URI led the country in scoring every year he was in school. His shots included a sixty-two-footer that tied the game and forced overtime in the 1946 NIT at Madison Square Garden against Bowling Green, a shot the New York newspapers dubbed, "The Shot Heard Round the World."

Calverley played professionally with the Providence Steamrollers and then spent sixteen years as URI coach, compiling a 154–125 record from 1952–68. His teams won four Yankee Conference titles and twice earned NCAA berths. He moved from coaching into the administrative offices and served as associate AD until his retirement in 1985.

11. Vinny Pazienza

He earned the title as the greatest boxer in Rhode Island history by winning seven world championships during his career, in the lightweight, light middleweight, and super middleweight divisions.

He did it all with a flair and a style that made him one of the biggest names in the nation in his prime, earning him the nickname "The Pazmanian Devil." He finished his career with a 50–10 record, including thirty knockouts.

Pazienza, who later changed his name to Vinny Paz, did it all despite suffering a broken neck in a serious automobile accident in 1991. Doctors told him he might never walk again, never mind box. He had to wear a medical halo for three months, with screws holding his brace in place.

Helped by a demanding workout regimen, the Cranston resident defied the odds. He not only returned to the ring thirteen months later, he defeated future world champion Luis Santana in a ten-round decision, completing a comeback some have called the greatest in boxing history.

12. Lou Gorman

A baseball lifer, Gorman became a respected Major League Baseball administrator with nearly a half century of work in the game.

The Providence native worked his way up the ladder of professional ball, beginning with a job in 1962 as general manager of the Class D Lakeland Giants. Within two years, Baltimore hired him to work in its front office as assistant director of its farm system. He went from the Orioles to Kansas City, eventually becoming assistant general manager in 1976.

He went from there to the Mets and finally returned home as Red Sox vice president and general manager in

1984. Gorman worked in various positions in the Boston organization until his death in 2011.

The only years he was not in baseball came when he spent eight years in the navy, which included two tours in Korea.

13. Ernie DiGregorio

He has lived one of the great Cinderella stories in the state's sports history.

He made a name for himself excelling as a star for the public high school in his hometown of North Providence. He went to college down the street from his home at Providence College and combined with fellow Rhode Islander Marvin Barnes to produce some of the greatest basketball in school history under coach Dave Gavitt.

DiGregorio, or Ernie D as everyone calls him, put on shows with his dazzling passing exhibitions as he help guide the Friars to the Final Four in 1973.

He was taken with the third pick in the 1973 NBA draft and lived up to expectations, becoming the NBA rookie of the year in 1974. Among other accomplishments, he led the NBA in assists and in free-throw shooting, at 94.5 percent, in the 1976–77 season. A severe knee injury cut his career short. He has been involved in numerous businesses in and around Rhode Island ever since and remains one of the most popular athletes the state has ever seen.

14. Lou Lamoriello

The Johnson native taught briefly at the high school in his hometown after graduating from Providence College, but gave it up to become involved in the sport he excelled at: hockey. It was a good decision. He is now in the Hockey Hall of Fame.

Lamoriello became the head coach of the hockey team at PC and stayed in that job until 1983. His last season his team went 33–10, the best record in the nation, and reached the Frozen Four.

The previous year, Lamoriello had been named athletic director at the school, so he focused on that job. In that role, he was among the founders of the Hockey East Conference and was named its first commissioner. The trophy given the champion each year is named in his honor.

In 1987, Lamoriello accepted a job as president of the NHL's New Jersey Devils. He spent twenty-eight years with the Devils, serving as general manager as well as president. His teams made the playoffs twenty-two times and reached the Stanley Cup finals five times, winning three. He was presented the Lester Patrick Trophy for outstanding service to hockey in 1992 and served as general manager for Team USA in both the 1996 World Cup of Hockey and the 1998 Olympics.

He is now the general manager of the Toronto Maple Leafs.

15. Hank Soar

It was his ability as a football player that made Soar famous and his work while serving in the army in World War II that led to a long career as an American League umpire. Soar attended Pawtucket Senior High, now Tolman, and Providence College before leaving to play semi-pro in both baseball and football.

He was picked up by the New York Giants and played in the NFL for the Giants from 1937 to 1946, working as both a running back and defensive back. He caught the game-winning touchdown pass in the 1938 NFL Championship game against the Packers in the Polo Grounds. While in the army during World War II, his work umpiring a baseball game caught the eye of Philadelphia Athletics manager Connie Mack. That led to a career as an umpire in the American League from 1950 to 1971.

He worked five World Series, including the 1969 meeting of the Mets and the Orioles.

16. Marvin Barnes

In terms of unpredictability and vast amounts of talent, Barnes might be number one in Rhode Island's sports history. There has never been anyone like him and likely never will be another.

The basic facts for the six-foot-eight basketball forward are that he is one of the greatest players ever in Providence College history, putting himself among the leading rebounders and scorers in school history as he and Ernie DiGregorio led the Friars in the NCAA Final Four in 1973. Among other accomplishments, Barnes led the nation in rebounding in 1973–74. He became the first player ever to go ten for ten in an NCAA Tournament game, and he once scored fifty-two points in a game against Austin Peay.

In the pros, he was the ABA rookie of the year in 1974–75 for the Spirits of St. Louis. He once had twenty-seven field goals in an ABA game and later played for four teams in the NBA, including the Celtics.

The problem was that he had major personal problems, beginning when he was part of a gang that robbed a bus while he was in high school. He was identified because he was wearing his Central High State Championship jacket with his name on it. Later in life, he had numerous drug problems and was homeless for a time. He died in 2014.

17. Mark van Eeghen

His ten-year NFL career was marked by two Super Bowl appearances with Oakland. The Cranston native excelled at Cranston West and Colgate before becoming the Raiders fullback.

He was something of an anomaly on the rough and tumble Raiders as a clean-cut, hard-working, straight-forward economics major in college.

He had no trouble fitting in with his team. He piled 6,651 yards rushing and added 174 receptions for 1,583 yards in his career. He had 5,907 of the rushing yards with Oakland, making him the Raiders all-time rushing leader when he retired. He totaled forty-one touchdowns in his career, which ended with the Patriots.

He was the leading rusher in Super Bowl XV with seventy-three yards on eighteen carries. He was an All-Pro selection in 1977.

18. Monk Maznicki

He went from an All-State football player at West Warwick High, to an All-American at Boston College, to an All-Pro for the Chicago Bears.

The West Warwick native was the running back on the 1941 BC team that won the Cotton Bowl. He was a third-round draft choice of the Chicago Bears in the then-new National Football League and earned All-Pro honors in his rookie year in 1942. He entered military service after that and was gone for three years, serving as a Navy pilot. One of his squadron mates was Ted Williams.

Maznicki returned to the NFL and helped the Bears win the World Championship in 1946. He returned to West Warwick, where the street he lived on was named after him: Coaches Court. He coached football and baseball for the Wizards for thirty-six years. His teams won seventeen divisional championships.

19. Ron Wilson

He was born in Canada but came to Rhode Island as a child, when his father became coach of the Rhode Island Reds.

He has been involved in hockey at every level, including international competition where he has taken advantage of his dual citizenship and coached for both the United States and Canada.

A high-scoring defenseman, he excelled at East Providence High and Providence College before playing professionally for twelve years in Europe as well as North America. His coaching career included two decades in the NHL, most notably with San Jose and Toronto.

He also coached the United States to a bronze medal in the IIHF World Championships in Vienna, the United States first medal in that event in thirty-four years. He was the head coach of the US Olympic Team in 2010, which finished second to Canada.

20. Bill Belisle

He is perhaps the greatest of the many high school coaching legends in the state. He never left home but impacted hockey at many levels.

He grew up in the Manville section of Lincoln and still lives there. His only break was to serve in the Korean War. He began coaching in 1954 and has spent more than sixty years doing it, most notably at Mount St. Charles Academy, where his teams won a national record twenty-six straight championships from 1978 to 2003. He has won more than nine hundred games, more than any high school hockey coach in history.

His former players include Brian Lawton, Bryan Berard, Garth Snow, Keith Carney, Mathieu Schneider, Eddie Lee, Brian Boucher, and Jeff Jillson, all of whom played in the NHL.

21. Mike Tranghese

After spending the first part of his career working as Dave Gavitt's right-hand man, Tranghese became a power in college athletics on his own merits.

He came to Rhode Island in 1972 as sports information director under Gavitt at PC. When Gavitt helped found the Big East in 1979, he brought Tranghese with him as his associate commissioner. The two worked together until 1990, when Gavitt left. Tranghese had made such an impression by then that he was selected to take over for Gavitt.

In a time when college sports began seeing major changes in conference alignments, Tranghese helped maintain the conference's position of national power, extending the Big East's impact to football. Tranghese became so involved and respected in football that he was named lead administrator of the Bowl Championship Series.

22. Mike Roarke

The West Warwick native spent his life involved in sports.

After a great high school career in football and baseball at West Warwick, he played both sports at Boston College and was captain of both in his senior year. He spent four seasons as a catcher with the Detroit Tigers. He then spent the next twenty years as a pitching coach, most notably with the St. Louis Cardinals when they won two pennants in the 1980s. He is credited with working with Bruce Sutter as Sutter became the first pitcher to effectively use a split-fingered fastball that made him one of the top relievers in the majors.

He finished his career spending three years as pitching coach for the Pawtucket Red Sox from 1981–83.

23. Joey Hassett

The son of one of the state's great high school basketball coaches, he has become one of the state's legends in the game himself through both his playing and his broadcasting.

A great outside shooter who earned the nickname Sonar early in his career, the Providence native excelled at La Salle Academy and then at nearby Providence College, where he became one of the few players to score at least five hundred points in three straight seasons. He played on the United States team in the 1975 Pan Am Games and was drafted in the third round of the 1977 NBA draft by Seattle. He helped the Sonics win the NBA title in 1979 before finishing his career with Indiana, Dallas, and Golden State.

He returned to Rhode Island and built a successful business career in investment banking, although most know him better in his second job—as the color analyst on PC broadcasts, where he and John Rooke have partnered for more than two decades.

24. Chris Terreri

There are not many athletes who win the most valuable player award in a national championship even though their team lost in the title game. Terreri is one.

The hockey goaltender highlighted a sensational career at Providence College by setting an NCAA record with 102 saves in the two games in the Frozen Four in Detroit in 1985. The Friars edged Boston College 4–3 in triple overtime in the semifinals then fell to RPI, 2–1, in the title game.

Terreri, who became one of the rare players who went to public school (Pilgrim High in Warwick) before playing Division I hockey, then went on to an excellent pro career, mostly with Lou Lamoriello's New Jersey Devils. Terreri played in the NHL for twelve years and was a member of two Stanley Cup winning teams. He finished with a 3.06 goals against average. He also represented the United States in the 1985 and '87 World Championship and in the 1988 Winter Olympics in Calgary.

He is currently the Devils goaltending coach.

25. Clara Lamore Walker

She was a Providence native who learned to swim at the Olneyville Boys Club and represented the United States in the 1948 Summer Olympics in London, competing in the breaststroke.

In the 1940s, she set two US swim records and won five national championships. She continued to swim for many years and became the world's dominant woman masters swimmer, setting records in numerous events. She was inducted into the International Swimming Hall of Fame in 1995.

26. Les Pawson

A Pawtucket native, he was one of the country's premier distance runners. His many honors included winning the Boston Marathon in 1933, 1938, and 1941.

He worked in the mills of Pawtucket and later for the City of Pawtucket. He died in 1992 at age eighty-seven.

27. Pat Abbruzzi

He was involved in football for more than five decades, starting as a player and finishing as one of the state's great high school coaches.

The Warren native set records at the University of Rhode Island in the 1950s, where he finished with a school record 3,389 yards and twenty-five touchdowns. He was drafted by the Baltimore Colts of the NFL but chose instead to go to Canada, where he excelled for the Montreal Alouettes for four years. He was named the CFL's most outstanding player in 1955 when he rushed for 1,248 yards (an average of 6.9 yards per carry) and seventeen touchdowns.

When he finished playing, he returned to his alma mater, Warren High, where he coached for twenty-six years and won eight division titles.

28. Billy Almon

The Providence native, who grew up in Warwick, remains to this day the only Ivy Leaguer ever selected first in the baseball draft.

Coming out of Brown University, Almon was the first overall pick in the 1974 draft by the Padres. He ended up playing fourteen years in the big leagues, compiling a .256 average, including .316 in his rookie year. A natural shortstop, he played every position except pitcher and catcher. He played for eight teams before retiring in 1988.

He later returned to his alma mater and coached the Brown baseball team for three years in the 1990s.

29. Gerry Philbin

A former Tolman High star, he became the first Rhode Islander to win a Super Bowl when he helped Joe Namath and the Jets upset the Colts in Super Bowl III.

A defensive lineman, he was twice selected as a first-team all-AFL player. That was in 1968 and '69, when he also was named to the All-Star team. He later played for the Eagles and in the World Football League.

30. Halsey Herreshoff

He is the best known as one of the many in the Ocean State who have been involved in ocean racing.

Among other roles, he was a yacht designer, and his Herreshoff Freedom 40 design became one of the most prominent in the world. He also sailed in America's Cup competition, including as a bowman on Columbia in 1958 and as navigator on Liberty in 1983.

He founded the America's Cup Hall of Fame, which is housed at the Herreshoff Marine Museum in Bristol.

31. Clem Labine

He was one of the Brooklyn Dodgers "Boys of Summer." Robert Creamer of *Sports Illustrated* labeled him "The King of the Bullpen."

A Lincoln native who grew up in Woonsocket, he was a standout relief pitcher for the Dodgers in their glory days of the 1950s. At one point, he held the National League career record for saves, all compiled from 1958 to 1962. When he retired, his ninety-six saves ranked him fourth in Major League history. Those do not include the 1956 and 1957 seasons, when he compiled nineteen and seventeen saves, respectively. At that point, saves were not yet an official category.

Labine had one victory and a save in four appearances as he helped the Dodgers win their first World Series in 1955. That year, he led the NL in appearances with sixty. Labine later pitched for Detroit and Pittsburgh and finished with the Mets. Overall, he worked in 513 games and had a record of 77–56 with a 3.63 ERA. He also worked in thirteen World Series games with a 2–2 record and 3.13 ERA.

He was twice an All-Star and three times a World Champion. He was the subject of a book written by lifelong friend Richard Elliott, *Always a Dodger,* published in 2015.

32. Bryan Berard

Injury brought an early end to what was developing as an outstanding NHL career.

The Woonsocket native was another in the long line of standouts to come out of the Mount St. Charles program. He was so good that he was the first overall pick by Ottawa in the 1995 NHL entry draft. He declined to report to the Senators and was traded to the Islanders. He played for four years, which was broken up by time away to play for the United States in the 1998 Olympics.

A defenseman, Berard piled up thirty-one goals and one hundred assists in 242 games. Shortly after being traded to Toronto, he was struck in the right eye by a stick, causing severe injury. He underwent seven surgeries on the eye and returned to play, although he never was able to return to the same level.

33. Sara DeCosta

A goaltender, she was a pioneer of sorts, not only playing ice hockey for the Toll Gate boys' team in Warwick, but excelling at it.

She played her college hockey at PC and was a star there, too, so good that she took some time off to represent the United States in international competition. Her work there included shutting out Canada in the 1997 Three Nations Cup, the first win ever for the United States over the Canadian women. It also was the first time Canada had ever been shut out.

From there, she went to the US Olympic team, where she helped the United States win a gold medal in the 1998 Olympics.

DeCosta continued her stellar play into the turn of the century and was named USA Women's Hockey Player of the Year in 2000. She has continued in the game running a hockey camp for girls. She also has worked as the goaltending coach at Harvard.

34. Dave Stenhouse

He went from the Rhode Island High school athlete of the year in 1951—he excelled in both basketball and baseball at Westerly High—to being the starting pitcher for the American League in the 1961 All-Star game.

Pitching for the Washington Senators, he had a 6–3 record and was battling for the league lead in ERA at the time. He finished the season 11–12 with a 3.66 ERA.

When his playing days were over, Stenhouse coached the Brown University baseball team from 1981 to 1990. His son, Mike, also played in the major leagues.

35. Brian Lawton

This Cumberland resident was perhaps the most heralded of the many great players produced by Bill Belisle at Mount St. Charles. He represented the United States in the World Junior Ice Hockey Championship in 1983 and played so well that he was the first overall pick in the NHL draft that year, taken by the North Stars. He was the first American high school player ever to earn that honor.

He played in 483 NHL games for six different teams over the next ten years. He scored 112 goals and added 154 assists, with his best season for Phoenix in 1990–91 when he had twenty-six goals and forty assists.

As soon as he retired, he formed a company to represent players, Lawton Sport and Financial. His clients included Mike Modano, Sergei Federov, and Ryan Malone.

He later moved into management and served as vice president of hockey operations for Tampa Bay and eventually as general manager and executive vice president of that team.

36. Robert Howard

He was a nine-team NCAA champion at Arkansas in the triple and long jumps and twice qualified for the US Olympic team, making the finals in both Atlanta and Sydney.

The former Shea High star did it all while taking pre-med courses with plans to be a neurosurgeon. He died tragically in 2004.

37. Steve Furness

A Warwick native, he stayed in Rhode Island for both high school, at Bishop Hendricken, and college at the University of Rhode Island.

He was selected in the fifth round of the 1972 NFL draft by Pittsburgh and went on to be one of the members of the Steelers' famed "Steel Curtain." He won four Super Bowl rings with the Steelers. He finished with thirty-two career sacks.

38. Harold "Chubby" Gomes

He was Rhode Island's first world boxing champion, capturing the Junior Lightweight title and the World Super Featherweight crown.

He won fifty-five of sixty-five career matches, including twenty-eight by knockout. At one point, he won twenty-two matches in a row. The Providence native fought his first match as a pro at age eighteen. After retirement, he remained involved in the sport as a manager, trainer, judge, and referee.

39. Tom Garrick

The West Warwick native went from almost being almost unwanted by Division I schools all the way to the NBA.

The guard combined with Silk Owens to form one of the greatest backcourts in URI history. Garrick finished in the top fifteen in Rhody history in points with 1,573, assists with 407, and steals with 189. Garrick was at his best in 1988 when the Rams advanced to the NCAA Sweet 16 before losing to Duke by one.

Among other work, he set a school record with fifty points in a victory over Rutgers in the Atlantic 10 Tournament. He then scored twenty-eight in an upset victory over Syracuse in the NCAA Tournament in Chapel Hill, North Carolina.

Along the way, URI became a national fan favorite because of Garrick and his father, Tom Sr., who attended the games even though he was blind, the result of being hit by a land mine in Germany during World War II.

Garrick was drafted by the Clippers and spent four years in the NBA, and then played five more years in Europe. He stayed in the game after retiring, coaching both men's and women's college teams at URI, Vanderbilt, and now Boston College.

40. Keith Carney

Hockey has been Keith Carney's life. The Providence native was one of the host of stars produced at Mount St. Charles under Bill Belisle.

He went to the University of Maine, twice helped the Black Bears to the Frozen Four, and was drafted in 1988 by Buffalo. He made his NHL debut in 1992 and spent the next seventeen years playing at the highest level. He played for six teams and in more than a thousand games.

A strong defenseman who was described as "an honest, basic defenseman, a cerebral rearguard," he piled up forty-five goals and 183 assists and finished his career with an awesome plus-164 rating. He played in the playoffs thirteen different seasons and had a plus-four rating there. He also played on the 1988 US Olympic team.

He currently serves as player development coach of the Blackhawks.

41. Tarzan Brown

He was one of the nation's great distance runners and one of the most unlikely stories of the century.

A Narragansett Indian born into poverty on the tribe's reservation in Ashaway in 1919, he was a natural distance runner. In 1936, at age eighteen, he showed up to run the Boston Marathon with old sneakers and a running outfit sewn together from a dress. At mile twenty-one, he tossed away his sneakers and ran the rest of the race barefooted, finishing thirteenth.

Brown, whose given first name was Ellison and whose Indian name was Deerfoot, won the Marathon in 1937 and 1939, when he became the first runner to break the 2:30 mark. He represented the United States in the Marathon in 1938 in Berlin, although he did not finish the race there. He was struck by a car and killed in 1975.

42. Dana Quigley

A Barrington native and URI grad, Quigley had what amounted to two careers. He dominated play among New England club pros through the 1980s and '90s. His titles included the RI Open six times and the Mass Open three times. He is co-record holder for winning the most NEPGA titles, with five.

At age fifty, he ventured out on the Champions Tour, which was then called the Senior PGA Tour. Competing as a Monday qualifier, he won the Long Island Classic on the same day his father, Wally Quigley, died. He became the tour's iron man, playing more than eight years (278 tournaments) without missing a start. He won eleven tournaments and more than $14 million.

43. Chet Nichols

This left-handed pitcher from Pawtucket finished second in the voting for National League rookie of the year in 1951. The guy who beat him was an outfielder named Willie Mays.

Nichols spent parts of nine seasons in the big leagues. His first was his best. He came so close to winning the rookie of the year award for the Boston/Milwaukee Braves because he was the National League earned run average champion.

Nichols finished his career with a 3.64 ERA in 189 appearances. His father, also named Chet, pitched in the majors from 1926-32.

Nichols is credited with being the person who suggested that one of his friends, a man named Ben Mondor, purchase the then bankrupt Pawtucket Red Sox franchise in 1977. Nichols then worked with Mondor in setting up what became one of the minor league's most successful franchises.

44. Wilma Briggs

One of eleven children who grew up on a farm in East Greenwich, she was introduced to baseball by playing family games on the farm.

She became the first girl to play on the high school boys' baseball team. After she graduated, she played in the All American Girls Professional Baseball League, the league made famous in the movie *A League of Their Own*.

A member of the Fort Wayne Daisies from 1948-53, she led the league in home runs in 1952, with nine. She finished second on the league's all-time home run list, with forty-three. When her playing career finished, she returned home, attended Barrington College, and taught at the Wickford Elementary School in North Kingstown until her retirement in 1992.

45. Curt Bennett

A member of one of Rhode Island's great hockey families— four members of the family played pro hockey—he has had an eclectic life.

He is an Ivy Leaguer, having gone to Brown University, where he set school records for goals by a defenseman in a game, season, and career. He was a Russian studies major and captain of the tennis team and was nominated as a Rhodes Scholar.

He was drafted by the St. Louis Blues in 1968 and played for the Blues and New York Rangers before going to the expansion Atlanta Flames. There, he was moved to forward where he twice made the All-Star team. He also represented the United States in the 1978 and 1979 Ice Hockey World Championships and finished his NHL career with 334 points in 580 games. He was the first American to score thirty goals in one season.

Among other work after finishing his playing career, he spent time in Japan in the 1980s helping coach players in that country. He currently lives in Hawaii.

46. George Patrick Duffy

He became a Rhode Island legend through his involvement with so many different teams and programs over an amazing seventy years.

The Pawtucket native was an excellent three-sport star in high school and then entered the service. While serving in the Coast Guard in World War II, the USS. Menges, on which he was serving, was torpedoed by a German U-boat in the Mediterranean Sea. He was seriously injured, but not only did he survive, he returned home and was involved in sports in Rhode Island through and even beyond the end of the twentieth century.

He was perhaps best known as both the broadcast voice of the Rhode Island Reds and the team publicist, as well. He traveled the American Hockey League circuit often by car and worked alone during games. Among his many other activities, he coached Little League baseball for years and guided his 1980 team into the Little League World Series. He also coached American Legion, CYO, Boys Club, and high school teams.

47. Mike Cloud

A Portsmouth High product, he had an All-American career at Boston College and then a five-year career in the NFL.

A running back at five foot ten and 205 pounds, Cloud set a BC record when he piled up 3,597 yards rushing in his four years that ended in 1998. He had fourteen touchdowns and 1,726 yards in his senior year alone and was named a first-team All-American.

He was selected in the second round (fifty-fourth overall) in the 1999 NFL draft and played for the Chiefs for four years before finishing his career with the Patriots.

48. Janet Moreau Stone

The Pawtucket native was Rhode Island's first gold medal winner in Olympic competition, earning it as a member of the 4-by-100 team in 1952 at Helsinki. She had narrowly missed making the 1948 Olympic team when she finished fourth in the 100 meters.

She competed in college for Boston University and earned a berth in the 1951 Pan-American Games. She spent her life after competition as a teacher at Pawtucket West (now Shea) High School.

49. Jimmy Van Alen

He was a fine tennis player himself, to the point where he won both singles and doubles in National Court Tennis. However, his fame was built off the court as one of the great promoters of the game.

He was the founder of the International Tennis Hall of Fame in his native Newport. Among the innovations he brought to the game was the Van Alen Streamlined Scoring System, the tiebreaker system used to this day to decide set winners. He was inducted in the Tennis Hall of Fame in 1965.

50. Julie Greene

When she was not teaching school—she taught at both the high school and college level—she was winning golf championships.

The Barrington resident captured eleven RIWGA Amateur Championships, more than anyone else in history, man or woman. Her many other titles included taking the New England Amateur twice, the Eastern Women's Amateur twice and that tournament's Senior Championship twice. In both 1975 and 1977 she reached the quarterfinals of the US Women's Amateur.

CHAPTER 25

NEWSPAPER CHANGES

There are not a lot of people left who remember when linotype machines were used to help print daily newspapers, nor are there many who remember discussions about the virtues of using "hot type" or "cold type" systems for publishing a paper.

I have been around long enough to have worked with both systems. And I remember dealing with proofreaders, who checked every story for typing mistakes before anything got into print.

In my last three years in the sports department at the *Pawtucket Times*, I acted as the editor at least one day a week. The paper was published six days each week. Ted Mulcahey put out the sports section most days. I did it on his days off.

Thinking of those days brings back bittersweet memories. We were still using typewriters and ripping out the pages when we finished a story. An editor would go over the story and literally write in corrections or changes he or she felt were needed. The paper then went to the linotype operator, who sat in front of a large machine and retyped the story, with small pieces of lead falling into place for each letter he typed. When he finished, ink was rolled over the surface to get a copy. That copy was sent to the proofreaders, who worked together in pairs to read each story and correct any mistakes. Anyone over the age of fifty will remember that it was extremely rare to ever see a spelling or grammatical mistake in a newspaper.

Once everyone was satisfied that there were no mistakes, the editor would go to the composing room—at the *Times,* it was one floor below the newsroom—and work with the pressman to make sure each story fit where it was supposed to according to the plan drawn by the editor. If it did not, it meant cutting out as much type as needed to make it fit or adding space bars between lines to extend the story as needed. By the end of the process in the hot-type system, each page could weigh close to a hundred pounds.

The basic system went back more than five hundred years to Johannes Gutenberg. Then everything changed in the 1960s and 1970s when a cold-type system, which made use of photo typesetting, was invented.

It made the work much easier, but it cost many jobs, as composing rooms were cut by 80 or 90 percent almost overnight. It was sad to see so many friends who did good work lose jobs. It also was only the start of job losses to computerization.

The changing technology played a huge role in my career. My big break came because of technology. In 1977, *The Providence Journal* joined the movement to total computer use. Typewriters disappeared.

Dick Reynolds, who had been the *Journal's* high school sports reporter for the previous four decades, was not ready to make such a dramatic change. Reynolds had become something of a legend in Rhode Island. He was a short, quiet, dignified man until he got in front of a microphone, when he became one of the funniest after-dinner speakers I ever heard. Much of his humor was directed at himself. He also was a walking encyclopedia on the development of the R.I. Interscholastic League. He knew everyone in the league, going back to pre-World War II days. For many years, the league did not have a full-time director, so Reynolds actually helped run the league.

By the 1970s, Reynolds had a daily routine. He would let Bill Troberman, Larry Gallogly, and a team of others answer the telephones to take game reports from around the state and write brief stories for the morning *Journal*. Reynolds, accompanied by his dog, would drive to Providence at 4:00 a.m., get a copy of the morning paper, and decide what he would write about for that day's evening paper. Reynolds himself would laugh at some of the reactions he received when he would call a coach at 4:15 or 4:30 in the morning.

Reynolds retired rather than switch from a typewriter to a computer. He told Gene Buonaccorsi, the sports editor, in July of 1977 that he was finished. Ed Duckworth, the assistant sports editor, recommended me for the job. On August 11, 1977, the day my son Jayson was born, I agreed to replace Reynolds as the *Journal's* high school sports editor.

Ever since, changes brought on by new technologies have come on a regular basis. We went through the use of scanners, portabubbles, the tiny Radio Shack desktop machines, and numerous other devices. Reporters had a front-row seat on the technological advances. When I began covering Red Sox games at Fenway Park, the old Associated Press tape machines were in the press box. They updated scores every half inning. With the advent of general access cable television in the 1980s, you no longer had to be in a press box to get updates on a game after each half inning. It was possible to sit at home and receive the same reports.

At the time, this all seemed incredible. Updates after every half inning while sitting in your den at home? Wow.

Today, that seems like the Dark Ages. Cable television brought about huge changes. But the advent of the Internet has had a far greater impact. Now, of course, we can see every pitch of every game with the statistics updated by the second.

A sportswriter's job today is far different than the one I lived through. And it is still changing, so much so that I have trouble when someone asks what my job was like. I can tell him what I did, but that is not much help, since anyone starting now will have a very different life with very different responsibilities.

There was a time when I would be asked to speak to a school group about my job, and I would be glad to tell everyone how much I enjoyed it. But everything was changing so much in the 1990s and 2000s that I reached the point where I shied away from speaking to students. All I could tell them was that the job today is very, very different than it was a generation ago.

The changes are not finished yet, not be a long shot. The Internet is still changing things. At the start of the century, the big change was that newspapers would put stories on the web even before the paper was published. There was no need to wait for the morning paper. The information was available before bedtime. The first experience I had along those lines was with Preston Murphy, a URI guard, from Saginaw, Michigan. He told me his mother was staying up until 11:30 or midnight on game nights because that was when the *Journal* put the URI game stories on the Internet.

She was in Michigan and could read the paper before someone who lived two blocks from the newspaper.

To this day, newspapers are still struggling to decide whether to make their pages available for free or whether to charge for the service.

For the writer, duties have changed dramatically. Writing a game story or a feature about one of the players is only part of the work and a relatively small part, at that. Virtually everyone at a newspaper of any size is asked to blog regularly. It is not enough to sit and listen to a Bill Belichick press conference anymore. There is a race among reporters to be the first to report news literally as it happens, either by blogging or by Tweeting. Belichick will smile at a press conference, and a half dozen reporters, newspaper guys, television people, and even those who work strictly for Internet sites, will dutifully report: Belichick just smiled.

The competition to report events as they happen affected how I did my job the last three years covering the Patriots. As with almost everyone who covered the team on a regular basis, I joined Twitter. As requested by sports editor Mike McDermott, I would Tweet events I thought were newsworthy and later add more detail in a blog. Everyone else would be doing the same thing. Writing a story for the newspaper often came after everything else was done.

All the Tweeting and blogging made for what I thought was a weird situation. Everyone follows everyone else on Twitter or Facebook or in blogs. So, when I Tweeted, I might have been helping someone from another paper, because he or she immediately saw what I was doing. It went in reverse, too, of course.

Mike Reiss of ESPN-Boston, one of the many newspaper guys turned Internet reporter, might have been the best in doing that work, especially when his two assistants, Field Yates and Mike Rodak, worked with him before leaving for other ESPN ssignments. They would do an amazing job keeping track of action. One might Tweet that Nate Solder, one of the Patriots tackles, just left the field and walked to the locker room. Another might Tweet that the Pats had switched their defense and had four safeties on the field. I was watching the game and trying to keep up with everything that was happening. But with Twitter, it was like I had twenty extra pairs of eyes, from all kinds of media, feeding me information that would help me do my job. It certainly did help me do my job.

I recommend to anyone who is interested in the subject to spend a Sunday afternoon following the Twitter action while watching any NFL game. Get the Twitter tag for a couple reporters for your favorite team and follow them. Soon, you will get the Twitter names for others on the beat and be able to get all the information you want on your team.

There also are negative aspects for a beat reporter to all the instant information. The Internet, as everyone knows, is not always correct. There are times when someone posts information that is wrong. There are times when that can lead to a call from an editor asking why the beat guy had not filed a report on that item. The reporter was to explain to the editor that the information he was asking about was wrong. You learn how much your editors trust you by how they react.

If you get the impression that I had mixed feelings about the way my job changed, you would be correct. The new duties were something I struggled with at times, as I'm afraid so many others of my era also struggle. On the other hand, the twentysomethings who do not know any other way love it. They deal with it much better.

Technological changes gave me my big break. And they helped make it an easy decision for me to retire in April of 2014.

Paul Kenyon acknowledges the crowd after being introduced during a time out at the final game he covered at the Ryan Center.

CHAPTER 26

THE PERSONAL TOP TEN

When every day is a good day at the office, it is difficult to single out some events as being the best. For what it's worth, when I am asked about special memories, these are the ones I place at the top of my list.

Everything is interchangeable, with one exception. There is no doubt about number one. I am eternally grateful for that one.

10. Rob Gronkowski at Trafalgar Square

It was spontaneous silliness, which is what made it special.

In normal weeks, the Patriots are sequestered the day before a game. It is part of getting prepared properly. However, when the team played in London in 2012, the schedule was dictated in large part by the NFL. One of the requirements was that each team would take part in a Fan Rally at historic Trafalgar Square. The Patriots did what was required, sending about a dozen representatives to fulfill their obligation.

Team owner Robert Kraft spoke about how the league was going to bring more games to Europe. Bill Belichick, who had indicated earlier that he was not thrilled to be on the other side of the Atlantic because it forced so many changes to his weekly schedule, proclaimed, "I love London." Tom Brady pointed to a number of Patriots jerseys in the crowd and said it looked as if it might feel like a home game.

Then Gronkowski stole the show.

When it was his turn to speak to the crowd of perhaps 1,500 fans, he began saying the normal things about how he was enjoying London. As he was speaking, members of the crowd began chanting "Spike the mic! Spike the mic! Spike the mic!" The radio disc jockeys that were the masters of ceremony for the rally began laughing. They looked at Gronkowski and smiled, in effect giving him permission to do what he wanted.

So Gronkowski did what he always does after scoring a touchdown. He spiked the microphone hard onto the stage. It bounced pretty hard. One of the disc jockeys went over and picked it up.

"It's broken," he said.

"I didn't think he'd really do it," the other disc jockey said.

The crowd roared. All the Patriots, including Belichick, laughed heartily.

The location made it even more special. Here it was in the center of London, in a square that often has been the scene of political demonstrations through the years, with the statue of naval hero Admiral Horatio Nelson hovering over everything surrounded by four large statues of lions. And there on stage was a smiling Rob Gronkowski, proud of what he had done.

He is what he is, a big kid who likes to have fun wherever he goes. His fun extended into the game. He scored two touchdowns as the Patriots romped over St. Louis. After the first, he marched stiff-legged like one of the guards who guard the queen at Buckingham Palace before doing his usual spike.

Whenever Gronkowski is involved, fun follows. For me, the mic spike was one of his best.

9. Patrick Horgan in the McCoy parking lot

The first big event anyone covers usually is special. It certainly was for me.

I moved from *Pawtucket* to the *Journal* in the summer of 1977 to cover high school sports. It was an era when school sports were still a main feature on the sports pages. With the help of John Gillooly, Bill Troberman, Larry Gallogly, Andy Catanzaro and a host of others, I made it through the fall sports season smoothly. It quickly became obvious that I would enjoy my new job.

When championship time came, I learned everything went up another notch. The *Journal* provided big-time coverage for the title events, especially the Super Bowls. I was as excited as the players from Rogers High in Newport and La Salle Academy in Providence when I covered my first Super Bowl in December of 1977. Both teams entered with perfect 9–0 records.

The game turned out to be a thriller. Rogers led most of the way, but La Salle scored a touchdown midway through the fourth quarter to take the lead, 17–13. Rogers got the ball back and proceeded to put together a drive an NFL team would be proud of, moving the length of the field and scoring the game-winning touchdown on a twenty-five-yard pass for a 20–17 victory.

The game was played in those days at McCoy Stadium in Pawtucket, the home of the Pawtucket Red Sox. As the Rogers players celebrated, we chased down winning coach John Toppa. Toppa was on his way to becoming a legend as one of the greatest high school coaches ever in the state. His teams won eleven state titles and thirteen divisional crowns in twenty-six years. Toppa, a gentlemanly, composed man, is now in the Interscholastic League Hall of Fame. When we began asking him about the game-winning drive, he deferred the credit to Patrick Horgan, the end who scored the winning touchdown.

"Give him the credit. He's the one who called it," Toppa said. We asked him to explain and Toppa spoke about how Horgan had come to him during halftime and suggested a play.

"He said they were playing him to the inside every time," Toppa related. "He said he was sure that if he faked inside and went outside, he'd be wide open." Toppa listened and put the idea in the back of his mind. His team was winning the game, so it kept doing what it had planned. However, when the Vikings fell behind, Toppa went to Horgan and asked if he was still being defended the same way. Horgan said he was.

With the game on the line, Toppa called the play. It worked perfectly. Horgan caught the pass and Rogers won the game. When we finished speaking with the coach, most of the Rogers players had left the field and gone to the team bus in the parking lot. I headed there and told the bus driver I needed Horgan. Horgan explained that it was nothing special, a simple down and out.

His coach often sought players' opinions on what was happening during a game, he said.

It all made for an easy story to write. I was happy that I had such a good story to tell in my first big chance to write what I knew would be a page one highlight. What made it even more memorable was that I have worked with Horgan—I call him Patrick, but many of his friends call him PH, as in Patrick Henry Horgan III—ever since.

Horgan went on to play both football and golf at the University of Rhode Island. Golf turned out to be his strength. He has played pro golf for the last thirty years, spending a decade on the PGA Tour. He now competes on the Champions Tour. He has become a good friend. I regularly remind him how he was the first big star I wrote about.

8. Jimmy Baron at Duke

For pure individual brilliance, the show Baron put on when URI played Duke in 2008 might have been the best I have ever seen on a basketball court. The fact that the game was played at Cameron Indoor Arena pushed the entertainment level up still another notch.

The game came about in large part because of Baron, the son of Jim Baron, who was then the URI coach. The younger Baron was a classic coach's son. He learned the game from his dad, who was a star himself at St. Bonaventure. He played with a knowledge and sense of the game beyond what most have. Jimmy Baron was much like his dad, not just a hard worker, but a zealot, a gym rat who outworked everyone.

One of his role models as a player was Duke's standout shooter, J.J. Redick. Baron had gotten tapes of Redick's workout plan at Duke and would copy the drills Redick and Chris Collins displayed in the tapes. Jim Baron had used his influence as a coach to speak with Duke's legendary coach Mike Krzyzewski and arrange the early-season game.

Even before Baron went wild on the court, the day was memorable for me. Cameron Indoor truly is a great place. The building, the team, and the way the Duke students put on a show of their own make it unique. When it came time to get to my seat before the game, I had to ask an usher for help. The Duke students pack the sidelines, so there is no room to walk to press row. The usher explained that reporters have to walk on the court itself, climb onto the press table, and then spin around and squeeze into their seats. All this, of course, is done while the place is going nuts with constant noise that lasts through the entire game.

The Duke students did not disappoint. Early on, they mocked Baron whenever he touched the ball, screaming "Daddy's boy! Daddy's boy!" One time, URI's backup center, Jason Francis, was fouled and went to the free-throw line. Francis was listed as six foot nine, 280, but probably weighed a bit more than that. He is a big guy. As he went to the line, the Duke students began a chant, "Please don't eat me! Please don't eat me!" Francis missed both free throws. I was convinced he was laughing as much as everyone else at the chant.

A funny thing happened as the game went on. Duke, then ranked eighth in the country, could not shake the Rams. Delroy James, the Rams' sleek forward, had a huge first half, on the way to scoring twenty-one points and helping Rhody lead 34–33 at the break.

218

The second half turned into "the Baron show." Baron had made one three-pointer in the first half. In the second half, he was nothing short of spectacular. He made three-pointers from the top of the key, from the corner, and from several feet beyond the arc. He took seven three-pointers and made every one of them. The Duke students went from mocking him to moaning every time he fired up another trey as he set a record for most three-pointers by a visiting player in the famed arena. Baron finished with twenty-four points, all on three-pointers.

"Baron had one of the greatest halves of any kid that's played against us," Krzyzewski said afterwards. "We were trying to figure out ways where he might not touch it."

Duke was behind most of the second half and needed the help of a couple questionable calls by the officials—the type of calls that always seem to go to the home team—to go ahead by one in the final minute. Baron had a chance to put URI ahead by one, but his fifteen-footer with five seconds left missed. Duke had shifted forward Kyle Singler, who is six foot seven, three inches taller than Baron, to guard him. Two later free throws by Duke made the final 82–79. It was Duke's sixty-second straight non-conference win at Cameron Indoor and as much fun at a basketball game as I have ever had.

7. Tiger and Annika win at Newport

Covering a national championship was special every time. But it meant even more when it was a "home" game.

Thanks to Newport Country Club, I was able to cover both a men's and women's national championship without leaving home. Both were beautifully run events that featured wonderful story lines

219

and great finishes, especially for those who like to see the best players play like the best. Tiger Woods won the second of his three US Amateurs in the centennial celebration held by the USGA in 1995, and Annika Sorenstam won what turned out to be the last of her ten majors when the US Women's Open was staged at the City by the Sea in 2006.

Newport Country Club truly is a special place. It still looks spectacular with its Whitney Warren-designed beaux arts-style clubhouse overlooking both the course and the Atlantic Ocean. The land was purchased in 1890 by a group headed by Theodore Havemeyer, the owner of the American Sugar Company, and others who owned mansions along Ocean Drive, including John Jacob Astor and Cornelius Vanderbilt II.

The first nine holes were built in 1894. Havemeyer, whose name is now on the trophy given to the Amateur champion, led the organization of a group of five clubs that founded the Amateur Golf Association in 1894, the group that turned into the United States Golf Association. It is one of the many beauties of golf that the same facility that hosted the first national championships was able to host the centennial event a hundred years later and could do it again today, if it so chose. History spills from every part of the club.

As we discussed in the earlier section on Tiger Woods, the centennial event turned into one of the first great exhibitions by the then nineteen-year-old Stanford sophomore. He was given a stern test by Buddy Marucci in the thirty-six-hole title match and won it, two up, after he hit an eight-iron within two feet for birdie on the final hole.

The Women's Open in 2006 was equally memorable. Sorenstam long since had established herself as the best player on women's golf and one of the best of all-time. She was on her way to winning seventy-two LPGA events, the third most ever, and another seventeen on the European LPGA Tour, the fifth highest total on that tour. Two years after winning at Newport, she retired from active competition at age thirty-six to start a family. She and her husband, Mike McGee, now have two children. Sorenstam has played rarely since retirement, although one of her starts involved a return to Rhode Island to compete in the CVS Charity Classic.

In Newport, Sorenstam tied Pat Hurst through seventy-two holes at even par 284. Sorenstam won the playoff, 70–74, for her third Open title.

I also got to work a third USGA Championship in Rhode Island, the 87th Women's Amateur at Rhode Island Country Club in 1987. Kay Cockerill, who has gone on to a career in television work, beat Tracy Kerdyk for the title in that one. It was Cockerill's second straight.

As much as the competition itself, I remember that one for the involvement of the people at RICC, headed by Audrey and Bob Sprague, who did such a great job in preparing and then running the tournament.

6. The Cooke family

A routine day at the State Amateur in July of 2011 turned into something very special. I will let the story I wrote for the Providence Journal explain it.

> WARWICK—When it was over, this match that was one of the strangest in the 106-year history of the R.I. Golf Association Championship, Tyler

Cooke was more worried about his father than himself.

The 19-year-old Cooke had just lost the biggest match of his young career, 2-and-1, to Bobby Leopold, his brother-in-law, at Potowomut. While he was disappointed, Cooke was more concerned with how his father was handling this highly unusual situation.

His father had just caddied in the match— for Leopold, his son-in-law. He has been doing that for several years now as he has helped turn Leopold into the best amateur golfer in the state. But this time was different because it meant he was working against his son.

"I think it was worse on him, to be honest. He was not good out there," Tyler Cooke said of his father. "It was the worst for him emotionally. It really hit him hard. Bobby and I are as close as they come with brother-in-laws. He's both of our dads now."

This was not a family feud.

In this one, no one was mad at anyone. The family is so close that having the brothers-in-law go against each other in the second round made it stressful for all involved, even more because it was on the home course for both players with numerous family and friends watching it all unfold. Taylor Leopold, Bobby's wife, was there watching her husband compete against her little brother.

"This feels so awkward," she said as she followed the match. "I don't know what to do."

Jean Cooke, Tyler's grandmother, was there too, as usual. She has spent a lot of time in the last several years cheering on Leopold as he has won numerous titles, including the championship of this tournament two years ago. The 81-year-old walked both qualifying rounds and then the first round Thursday morning.

"I don't care what happens," she said as she watched, this time while riding along in a golf cart. "I just want them both to play well."

It turned out that neither played as well as he had earlier in the week. Leopold led early by two holes, Cooke came back to pull even, then Leopold regained the lead and earned the 2-and-1 decision.

"It was the most nerve-racking experience of my life," Leopold said. "At some points I was struggling to take the club back. It was tough. I said to Scott on the first hole, 'I understand if you don't want to caddie. Tell me now and I understand completely.'"

"I didn't think it was going to be that hard," Tyler Cooke said. "I thought it was going to be friendly walking up and down the fairways. It really wasn't like that. After the first tee shot it was really awkward. No one wants to lose; losing sucks. I know he doesn't want to lose. He wants to win as bad as anyone right now. I'm the same way."

"It's tough to be all lovey-dovey when we all know what it means," Leopold said. "It means a lot to Ty and it means a lot to me. It was hard to just chat like you usually do with a normal playing partner. It was hard because I couldn't feed off Scott for energy ... It was the hardest round of golf I've ever played, harder than the qualifier for the US Am, harder than any of that."

When it was over, after everyone shook hands and began walking in from the 17th, Scott Cooke headed off by himself and walked in alone, still clearly unnerved because of the experience. At first he declined a request to talk about it, saying, "I just can't right now."

Sometime later, he felt ready to talk, but he was still choking with emotion. He had helped Leopold win, but he was having trouble dealing with opposing his son.

"Bob said it would be all right if I bowed out this afternoon, but I said, `Never leave your wingman.' Bob's like my son," Cooke said. "I'm not his father, but I'm pretty close. He's been part of our family a long time now. I've taken him under my wing. He's a great kid."

5. Jon Lester's no-hitter

As with any job, writers spend a good amount of time checking on what others in their position are writing about. You have to be aware of what the competition is doing. There are times when it can give you ideas of ways to do your job better. I found that so many had definite styles. Some guys love statistics and use the stats to explain what happens. Others focus heavily on relating as best they can the facts of what takes place.

In May of 2008, I remember spending an especially long time studying how everyone had handled Jon Lester's no-hitter against Kansas City. For me, the night could serve as an ideal illustration on my style. As I've mentioned so often here, for me, the people are even more fun than the game itself. The scene on the field after the last out turned into my focus for *Providence Journal* readers.

At Fenway, the press box is on the sixth floor. Writers at Fenway look down from directly behind home plate. When the last out is recorded, everyone heads down the hallway to the elevator. A special elevator is kept for reporters to take us down the six stories. We then fight the crowd, which is heading out, to go in and to the first-base side, where the Boston clubhouse is located. Those wanting to speak to the manager get off on the second floor and wait in the small press room there. Since the clubhouse is closed until ten minutes after the final out, there is plenty of time to be wherever you feel you need to be.

On this particular night, I hesitated after the final out. While most others rushed to get downstairs, I wanted to watch the on-field celebration. Manager Terry Francona, who is one of the good guys to work with, gave me more than I was looking for. He put what the night meant in perspective. Lester was returning from a battle with cancer. Francona had developed an especially close relationship with him. Here is my Journal story from that night:

> BOSTON—Terry Francona's reaction said it all. What Jon Lester did last night in pitching a no-hitter as the Red Sox beat Kansas City, 7-0 at Fenway Park was special, even by no-hit standards.
>
> When Lester had finished being carried by catcher Jason Varitek and being mobbed by his teammates, he worked his way over to his manager. Francona greeted him and acted a bit differently than most managers do in such situations. He took Lester's face in his hands, both hands, spoke to him briefly, then gave him a long hug. Finally, he spoke to Lester again before letting him go.
>
> It clearly was an emotional moment for both, different than manager and player. They were more like friends who had been through a difficult

situation together, specifically the rare form of non-Hodgkin's lymphoma Lester battled two years ago. It made this great moment even more special.

"With everything I've been through, he's been like a second dad to me," Lester said. "Just being able to talk to him, not as a manager but as a friend; he cares a lot about his players. It's not just about what you do on the field. It's what type of person you are. He cares a lot about that."

It completed a truly memorable day for Francona. He spent the first part of the day watching his son, Nick, graduate from the University of Pennsylvania.

"This probably isn't fair to say, but I feel like my son graduated and my son threw a no-hitter. It couldn't happen to a better kid," Francona said. "That's probably selfish on my part to even say something like that, but I think it's obvious how we feel about this kid."

"He's a wonderful kid not because he threw a no-hitter; he's a good kid because he's a good kid," Francona said. "We're proud of him all the time. To watch him do that tonight was beyond words. I'm trying to put it into words but it's beyond words. What a story. To see him do that, you feel like a proud parent. I know we have no right to say that, but it's probably how we feel."

Lester might be the quietest player on the Red Sox team. The native of Washington state goes about his business without fanfare. He is polite and soft-spoken. The fact that the 24-year-old not only has survived cancer, but has dealt with it so stoically has made him one of the team's most popular players.

Lester allowed only two base runners, a walk to Billy Butler in the third and a walk to Esteban German leading off the ninth. He threw a career high 130 pitches and struck out a season high nine.

As so often happens with a no-hitter, there was one special play to keep it alive. That came from center fielder Jacoby Ellsbury, who came in and toward right on a soft fly ball by Jose Guillen in the fourth and made a fabulous diving backhanded catch inches from the ground.

"It wasn't until after the catch that I actually realized he had a no-hitter," Ellsbury said. Boston led 5-0 at the time, thanks to a five-run third.

"It was nice having the cushion at the time and knowing that you can really lay it out," Ellsbury said. "I was just thinking, 'Go get it.' I knew J.D. (Drew) was backing me up, so in that situation I can really lay out for it."

Otherwise, Lester was in full control. He threw first-pitch strikes to 20 of the 29 hitters he faced. The fact that he pitched so well was a surprise only because he felt he warmed up badly.

"If you had seen me in the bullpen, you would have thought I wouldn't get out of the first inning," he said. On a cold night that made griping the ball difficult on breaking balls, he and catcher Jason Varitek, who became the first catcher ever to receiver four no-hitters, went more with a four-seam fastball.

"In the first inning, John (pitching coach John Farrell) and I were talking and commenting on how he was going back and forth, up and down, changing speeds, working quick, attacking the zone, but with different eye levels, different speeds, different planes," Francona said.

As Lester mowed down batter after batter, the sellout crowd of 37,746 got more and more into it. Lester, who also pitched the deciding game of the World Series last year, said he followed his usual routine in the dugout, which is to move around quite a bit so as not to sit and think too much. Francona, who insists he is not superstitious, was on this night.

"I didn't do a darned thing different. My shoe felt like it was going to fall off the last three innings, but I wouldn't tie it," he said. "I was glad we had some runs because you can watch a little more and get caught up with him."

The fans got caught up, too. By the ninth, flashes were going off all over Fenway on every pitch. When he struck out Alberto Callaspo for the final out, Lester raised both fists and celebrated until Varitek came out and lifted him off the ground, keeping him in his arms until everyone else came out and joined the celebration.

It was the 18th no-hitter in Red Sox history, the first by a lefty in Fenway since Mel Parnell in July of 1956.

It turned a cold night in May into a game to remember, although Lester said he was having trouble digesting it all.

"It really hasn't sunk in," he said. "Right now it feels like I pitched and we won the game. I think it's like the World Series. It takes a while for this to set in and give you time to reflect on it. I guess it's one of those things you get to enjoy later."

4. The Ryder Cup at Brookline

Those who do not follow golf will find it hard to believe, but as far as I am concerned, the events that took place at The Country Club in the 33rd Ryder Cup matches in September of 1999 made for one of the top five most exciting sports events I ever attended. It was unpredictable, totally out of character for golf and flat out thrilling.

A day that began with people poking fun at the shirts the United States team was wearing ended with the Americans rallying from a 10–6 deficit to a 14 ½–13 ½ victory, fulfilling a prediction made by team captain Ben Crenshaw the previous day. It was hard to take Crenshaw seriously when he predicted the rally, even more since the Americans had not won the matches against the European team since 1993.

But the most individual of games did indeed turn into an unforgettable team victory. Justin Leonard was the ultimate hero, capping a dramatic rally from four down through eleven holes to beat Jose-Maria Olazabal with a dramatic forty-five-foot birdie putt on the seventeenth green. The reaction by the Americans upset the European side because everyone ran on the green to celebrate, even though Olazabal had yet to attempt his putt. In many respects, the Europeans were correct. It was poor sportsmanship. But for those who were there, who lived through the emotion of the day, it was entirely understandable.

It was not just that Leonard had not won a match in his two Ryder Cup appearances. It was the excitement of the day when Tom

Lehman, Hal Sutton, Phil Mickelson, Davis Love III, David Duval, and Steve Pate all posted victories. The noise was deafening through the day as one American player after another won holes and the team made up a deficit that no other team ever had overcome. One of my assignments that day was to follow Duval's match against Jesper Parnevik. Duval was one of several Americans who had spoken before the matches about how disappointing it was that the participants did not get paid to play. It was Duval's first appearances in the matches.

Here is part of what I wrote after Duval won his match:

> BROOKLINE, Mass.—David Duval finally opened himself up to the world yesterday and it was nice to see what was inside.
>
> While every member of the American team had a right to celebrate after the historic comeback win in the 22rd Ryder Cup matches, no one did it any better or with any more vigor than Duval.
>
> There he was, the iceman of the PGA Tour, standing on the 14th green at The Country Club after he had just closed out his victory over Jesper Parnevik, pumping his fists in exultation. Duval turned to the fans on every side of the green, each time pumping both fists in the air.
>
> His shirt tail was hanging out. He was letting himself go, allowing himself to enjoy the moment. He was saluting the fans, bonding with them.
>
> Finally, he put his hand to his ear signaling for still more applause. He saluted the crowd and pumped his fists one final time.
>
> "I love it," he said later. "This is not like any other event."

It was the kind of emotional display that Tiger Woods and Sergio Garcia stage often. But it was something the 27-year-old Duval has never allowed himself to do since he began playing on the PGA Tour in 1993.

It was an exhibition that can change an entire career, and only for the better.

"This is, as many people have told me, something that you can't explain and you can't appreciate until you've been a part of it," Duval said after the celebrating had at least slowed down a little bit. "The great analogy I was given I that it's like when you have your first child. You can't explain it to anybody. You have to go through it."

This is the same Duval who said not long ago that the Ryder Cup was just an exhibition, that he was not all that excited about taking part; the same David Duval who was one of four American players who suggested that the participants should be paid for taking part.

Later, Duval spoke about how it was impossible not to get caught up in the emotion, especially when cheered on by a rowdy Boston crowd.

"I'm not going to retract some of the things about the money going for charity," he said. "But to feel the heat of it all, the magnitude and even the history of it, is something that I can't personally put into words. I don't have the vocabulary for that.

"It is," he said, "more than anything I've ever experienced."

3. Lamar Odom's shot

One of the lessons I learned immediately upon beginning to cover sports was that I had to separate my personal feelings from my job. I found that it was not hard to do.

When I was covering a game, especially at the start of my career when it involved high school teams, I had to devise my own system for keeping track of what was happening. In football and basketball, in particular, I had to keep track of each play and each player's statistics, because many of the schools did not do that. It was not tough to do, by any means, but it meant keeping busy and ignoring the emotions that fans have while rooting for their teams. Even after switching to the college and pros, I kept doing it because I felt it gave me a better feel for what was happening.

I can honestly say that I was able to simply do the work without rooting, even when it was the "home" team I knew well against a visiting team I barely knew at all. Of course, there were feelings when a player I liked did well. But I can honestly say I almost never openly rooted for any team during game action.

Almost never, I said. There were special times when the professional feelings were pushed into the background. The most dramatic one for me came in March 1999 at The Spectrum in Philadelphia.

URI, after having a solid but not special 17–12 regular season, romped over La Salle in the A-10 quarterfinals and then outscored George Washington in the semis to earn a spot against top-seeded Temple in the title game. Temple long had been a power in the conference under the great John Chaney. It already was assured of another berth in the NCAA Tournament. URI knew that it had to win the game to return to the NCAA Tournament, where it had reached the Elite Eight the previous season.

This URI team revolved around the immensely talented Lamar Odom, but also included holdovers Preston Murphy and Antonio Reynolds-Dean, two players who had fabulous careers in Kingston. Both are terrific young men who have remained involved in the college game as coaches. Before the game, I remember a conversation with Bill Reynolds, the *Journal* columnist who was covering the tournament with me, about what a fitting way it would be for Murphy and Reynolds-Dean to get to go back to the Big Dance.

But that seemed unrealistic. Temple had beaten URI by thirteen in their first meeting at Temple, then by nine in Rhode Island when URI was still playing some home games at the Providence Civic Center.

When the final began, the Rams played well, and Jim Harrick showed what a good game-day coach he was. The teams went back and forth and were tied in the final minute. Temple missed a shot with ten seconds left. Odom rebounded and brought the ball to midcourt, and the Rams called a time out with six seconds remaining. Harrick did not have to be a great coach to set up what happened when play resumed. He had his team get the ball inbounds to Odom near midcourt. Odom moved up the left side, and then, as he reached the URI bench, rose and fired a shot from about thirty feet out. It swished through as the final buzzer was sounding.

I have to confess that it was the first and only time I cheered while sitting in the second row of the press section. I was happy for everyone involved with the program at my alma mater.

Then I was almost scared to death seconds later. As we were watching the URI players pile on top of Odom, who had run to the opposite end of the court, a big man landed on the press table between Reynolds and me, shaking the table. The man then jumped over the front row and onto the court. Some of the pictures of the celebration include him on the pile.

It was Carl Koussa, one of the most fervent of URI fans for the last forty years, a guy who regularly attended road games as well as home games. It also was the only A-10 title the URI men's team has won to this day.

2. Super Bowl XXXVI

As I discussed in the Patriots section at the start of this book, the Super Bowl truly is the great American show, the best sporting event I have had the chance to witness. But even by Super Bowl standards, this one was special. It culminated perhaps the busiest, most hectic three-week stretch of work ever for me.

Actually, it was not just the three weeks leading up to the Super Bowl. It was the entire season.

The Patriots began 0–2 and lost their quarterback, Drew Bledsoe, to injury in a loss to the Jets in week two. That brought in a second-year guy, a sixth-round draft choice named Tom Brady. Brady was a pleasant surprise as he played well and led the Pats to an 11–5 record and a spot in the playoffs.

It all happened during a season interrupted by the tragic 9/11 attacks. All games were called off in the aftermath of the attacks, pushing the schedule back one week and backing the Super Bowl, which was to be played in New Orleans, into February for the first time.

In the playoffs, the Patriots met Oakland in the Divisional Round in what was to be the last game ever at old Foxboro Stadium. It came to be known as the "Snow Bowl" when heavy snow fell during the game. It also became known as the "Tuck Rule Game."

Oakland appeared to have won when Charles Woodson sacked Brady late in the fourth quarter with the Raiders on top, 13–10. The hit forced a fumble, which the Raiders recovered. As Oakland was celebrating, the play was reviewed, and referee Walt Coleman invoked a little-known rule that the play was actually an incomplete pass because Brady had begun the throwing motion and then tried to tuck the ball away when he saw the defender coming at him. (It is a rule that was later revoked by the league.)

New England was able to keep the ball and move far enough down field to allow Adam Vinatieri to kick a forty-five-yard field goal into the driving snow, a kick Vinatieri has called the best of his career. The Patriots went on to win on another Vinatieri field goal, this one a more modest twenty-three yards, in overtime.

That gave the Pats a berth in the AFC Championship game the following Sunday in Pittsburgh. It created an unusual situation for the reporters. There would be no week off between the conference title games and the Super Bowl. Thus, we had to fly to Pittsburgh with ten days worth of clothes. We all made tentative airline reservations both to fly back home after the game or to fly from Pittsburgh to New Orleans either Sunday night or first thing Monday morning to get there for the start of Super Bowl happenings. For some reporters, it did not matter, because they were going regardless of which team won in Pittsburgh. For the *Providence Journal,* it made all the difference. If the Patriots lost, we were heading back home.

The Steelers were favored to win. I remember conversations with other New England reporters about what a pain it was to pack so many clothes when the expectation was that we would be returning home, not going to New Orleans.

The Patriots got off to a good start in the game thanks to a Troy Brown punt return for a touchdown. But in the second quarter, Brady was injured and the almost-forgotten man, Bledsoe, returned to action. Bledsoe, who had been ready for some time, had played the good soldier. He sat and watched Brady run the team. Bledsoe never publically complained.

Bledsoe played well, had a touchdown pass to David Patten, and was the hero as the Pats won, 24–17. After the game, we wrote our stories around making calls to make sure we had flights to New Orleans and a hotel room to stay in.

The veteran reporters had told stories about how they were selfishly hoping the Patriots would win because New Orleans is, in their opinion, the best place to hold the Super Bowl. Work is easy because everything is so close together. And New Orleans is the perfect party town to host all the festivities that go along with the game.

They were correct, I learned. It was a great week, with work made easier than ever because of all the transcripts provided to reporters. The parties went on every night, and the food, well, there is no place any better.

The game provided the ultimate finish. The Patriots refused to be introduced individually and instead came out as a team, adding to the emotions. The Pats slowed the heavily favored St. Louis Rams and their "Greatest Show on Turf." Even halftime was superb, with the band U2 putting on a sensational show. With the game at night, we had to do work at halftime. But U2 was so good that many of us paused to enjoy the show.

The Patriots provided one of the most exciting finishes in Super Bowl history, led by Brady, who had been given his job back. After the Rams had tied the game late in the final quarter, the Pats refused to just sit on the ball and wait for overtime. Brady led a drive that got the Pats far enough down field to allow Vinatieri to kick a forty-eight-yard field goal that gave the Pats their first Super Bowl.

With more follow-up work the next day, including the press conference with Brady, the game MVP, I believe it made twenty-two straight days of work without a break. And I loved every minute of it. It was one of the highlights of my working life.

1. 9/11/2000

In contrast to Super Bowl XXXVI, this was a game almost no one remembers. It was the second week of the season in Bill Belichick's first year as New England coach. The Jets scored two touchdowns in the fourth quarter to come from behind and edge the Pats, starting a slide that would send New England to a 5–11 record, the last losing season the team has had.

I remember it because it saved my life, thanks to the doctors at the Hackensack University Medical Center.

I will say it one more time. I've been a lucky man. And this was the luckiest of all the lucky days I have had. Had I been home on that night, I would have gone to bed and never awakened. Instead, the NFL schedule maker, my friends Jim Donaldson and Kevin Mannix, a security guard, and a doctor at The Meadowlands and the wonderful doctors and nurses at the Hackensack Medical Center saved my life.

To explain: When I had assignments in the New York City area, I preferred to drive. Others preferred to fly. For this Monday night game, I drove to the Newark Airport Marriott, arrived in midafternoon, checked into the hotel, and got ready for the game. Donaldson, our columnist for the *Journal*, and Mannix, the gentlemanly beat reporter for the *Boston Herald*, met me there. As we had arranged earlier, I drove them to the game.

Everything was normal until halftime. When I finished sending some notes on what took place in the first half, I got up to go to the bathroom and get something to eat. When I did, I felt nauseous. I felt as if I was going to vomit, to the point that I did not get anything to eat. When I returned to my seat, I told Jim that he might do well to move. I was getting sick. There was no chest pain at all. It felt like the onset of the flu.

The game went on, and the Jets rallied to win. I started to head to the locker rooms to do the usual interviews, but I was just too ill. When Jim came back, he gave me a couple quotes to insert into my stories, and I did the best I could to finish my work.

The press parking at the old Meadowlands Stadium was a good distance away from the entrance. So, as we were heading out at about 1:00 a.m., I suggested that Jim or Kevin get the car while I waited at the entrance. They looked at me and said we should get help. As they were saying so, we passed a security guard. They asked if the medical staff was still in the stadium. The security guard made a call on his radio and was told a doctor was still there. He made arrangements to have a cart pick me up and take me to the medical office.

When I told the doctor there what was happening, he reached into a cabinet, gave me a small pill, and told me to put it under my tongue. Within seconds, I felt much better. It was nitroglycerin. I thanked him and started to get up. The doctor had other ideas.

"This man is having heart issues. Take him to Hackensack," he told the technician.

The Hackensack University Medical Center is not the usual hospital where patients are sent. As I learned later, it has one of the best heart centers in the nation.

I gave Jim my keys. He drove Kevin back to the hotel. I vaguely remember Jim stopping in at the hospital sometime in the early-morning hours. He and Kevin were great. I only half kiddingly call them my guardian angels. If they had not done what they did, I would not be here. The doctors explained that many people go through what I went through that night. They feel sick, so they go to bed—and they never wake up. One of my cousins, Chuck Kenyon, had the same thing happen to him. Ironically, it happened on the night of the Patriots' second Super Bowl appearance. He went to a party near his home in Virginia, felt ill, went home, and never woke up.

I was at a point in my career where I was gone only twenty-five to thirty nights year. If it had happened any of the other 335 nights, I would have died. To this day, I wonder why everything happened as it did and I'm still here.

I am still here because of the doctors and nurses at Hackensack, who were absolutely spectacular. They put together a team that performed an emergency triple bypass on the morning of September 11. I remember almost nothing except a nurse comforting me as I was headed into surgery. The doctors later told my wife that as I was having a procedure done, I had a massive heart attack. If I had been anywhere else except on the operating table, it would have killed me. They also told her that there was evidence that I had had three previous smaller heart attacks.

My wife and sons spoke afterward about how much help they received in the following days, how they were overwhelmed by the kindness shown. I've mentioned here several times about how lucky I was to work at the *Journal*, and that was never truer than in the days following the surgery. Art Martone, our sports editor and one of the best people I ever worked with, kept in contact and even volunteered to go to New Jersey if help was needed. Howard Sutton, the publisher, personally became involved and made sure my family had everything it needed. Jim Donaldson contacted my wife at her office as soon as he returned to Rhode Island. He updated her on my situation and told her she needed to go to New Jersey. He and Martone made arrangements for plane tickets for my sons and wife to fly to Newark. The doctor contacted them as they were packing to tell them that I was headed to emergency surgery.

After the first night, the hotel my family was staying in said they had a big group coming in and would not have room for them, so they had to move. When the people at the *Journal* found out, including the terrific Carol Montrond, the person who helped us with all our travel arrangements, they jumped in. Kevin McNamara, who already had established himself as one of the best college basketball writers in the country, used his ties with the Marriott Hotel rewards program to arrange a move to a new hotel.

Don Kaull and Steve McDonald, the URI broadcasters, called and offered help. Al Skinner, the URI coach who had been such a huge help in getting my college work started, called several times to ask how I was doing and offer help. This was after Skinner had left for Boston College. I no longer had any contact with him and likely never would again. But it spoke about the character of the man that he took time to offer support and encouragement, even to the point of being one of the first to reach my room when I was able to speak. Sean McAdam, the *Journal's* lead baseball writer, came in with his two children, Liza and Connor, when visitors were allowed. So many people were so good to us.

I ended up spending two weeks in the hospital. There were complications following the surgery. I came down with C. difficile, a disease that brought on terrible vomiting and becoming ill simply by smelling food. Through it all, the help I received at the hospital was nothing short of outstanding.

As the years passed, I came to appreciate what they did for me more than ever. I saw my sons grow into good men who make Pauline and I proud. They have wonderful partners in life in Aimee and Cheri. And they have given us three beautiful grandchildren in Daniel, Charlotte, and George. I've seen my sister, Patricia, someone who has spent her life helping others as a schoolteacher, find happiness with her marriage to Bob Mancuso.

The experiences have given me a different perspective on life, an ability to appreciate each day.

Since I've been back home, Dr. John Solomon, our family doctor, Dr. Kenneth Korr, who took over as my cardiologist, Dr. Peter Soukas, who performed more surgery several years ago to allow me to walk better, and Dr. Hilary Whitlatch, my endocrinologist who has guided me at the Hallett Diabetes Center, all have helped keep me going. I can't thank them enough.

I have spent my life writing and giving credit to athletes playing games. Hopefully, it has provided entertainment for the readers.

Sports are an important part of our society. But what happens in athletics pales in comparison to what medical people do. I can't imagine the feeling a person has when he or she saves a life, as they did for me. They are the ones who should be singled out for what they do every day.

I was embarrassed that I did not even remember the names of the doctors and nurses who saved my life at Hackensack. Finding out and thanking them publically became one of the biggest reasons I decided to write this book. With all the HIPPA requirements these days, it is not easy to go back sixteen years and find out who cared for me. Back then, everything was on paper. The paper has long since been put away and been replaced my computers. With the help of Nancy Radwin and Ryan Ullman, I was able to get their names.

The surgeon who performed the bypass was Dr. Elie Elmann. He was assisted by Dr. James McFarland. The anesthesiologist was Dr. Lawrence Abrams, and the scrub nurses were Mila Arce, Agnes Kim, Diane Waeapy, and M. Mardon. The recovery-room nurses were Julie Every and Christina Rifflard.

Those were the people who saved me in the first hours. There were many, many more that cared for me in the next two weeks. As I think about everything I went through and all the help I received, it all is very humbling. I spent my life making a big deal about people playing games and receiving millions of dollars and tons of attention while doing it. I truly was fortunate to be in the right place at the right time in so many different ways and be able to meet and work with so many great people.

At the same time, there are so many others, like the doctors and nurses who cared for me, who do it all for much less compensation and with much less attention. Yet, I remember the atmosphere in the hospital as being tremendously upbeat and positive. The medical people obviously do it because they enjoy it.

One of the reasons I got into sportswriting was because of advice I received from my father, George. He spent his life working for the post office, at the stamp and money-order window. He did it for more than thirty years and loved it. He knew everyone in town, and they knew him. He loved people and loved keeping up with everything going on in town.

"I don't care what you do when you grow up," he told me many times, "but you better do something you enjoy. The most important thing is enjoying what you do. You have to be able to look forward to going to work when you wake up every morning."

He was so right, of course. I truly did enjoy going to work. But what I contributed was nothing compared to what the doctors and nurses do every day. I'm in awe of what they have done for me and for so many others. Thank you so very much to everyone for making it such a great life.

I am a lucky man.

CPSIA information can be obtained
at www.ICGtesting.com
Printed in the USA
FSOW01n1737181216
28729FS